How Does a Christian Profit from Tough Economic Times?

How Does a Christian Profit from Tough Economic Times?

What to Do about the
Great Recession as a Christian

VAL J. PETER

Boys Town, Nebraska

How Does a Christian Profit from Tough Economic Times?

Copyright © 2011 by Val J. Peter

ISBN 978-1-934490-24-2

Printed and bound in the United States of America.

Boys Town Press is the publishing division of Boys Town, a national organization serving children and families.

Publisher's Cataloging-in-Publication Data

Peter, Val J.

How does a Christian profit from tough economic times? : what to do about the great recession as a Christian / Val J. Peter. -- Boys Town, Neb. : Boys Town Press, c2011.

p. ; cm.

ISBN: 978-1-934490-24-2

Includes bibliographical references.

1. Economics--Religious aspects--Christianity. 2. Global Financial Crisis, 2008-2009--Religious aspects--Christianity. 3. Recessions--Religious aspects--Christianity. 4. Christianity--Economic aspects. 5. Spiritual life--Christianity. I. Title.

BR115.E3 P48 2011

261.8/5--dc22   1104

TABLE OF CONTENTS

PREFACE

Many Americans are uneasy about the current economic downturn, as well as our still-affluent way of life compared to the poor of the world and even the poor we have in our own country. On one hand, they want to avoid a lack of sensitivity to the poor. On the other hand, they want to avoid a neurotic view of their lifestyle.

Here is a book that can be of great help to you in this regard.

This little book combines two very, very important stories.

The first story is about the economic collapse worldwide that started in 2007 and is still center stage, not just in the United States but worldwide. The economic collapse, on one hand, tells the story of the bold dream of economic growth through ever-changing, ever-new complex financial products, corrupted by Wall Street greed that unleashed this catastrophe. That's the story from the top – wealthy financiers who cut corners and lined their own pockets. The other part of the story is the discovery of how the working poor became big business in predatory schemes.

Then there is ancient Christian wisdom that looks at the world of material goods through the Centuries as cultures and economics and business change. Basic Christian wisdom does not change in its essentials, but adapts itself to the times.

There is a real benefit in reading a book like this. It raises questions. It calls to action and, above all, it invites you to pray for wisdom in doing so.

Happy reading.

Father Steven Boes
President and National Executive Director
Boys Town

INTRODUCTION

Beginning in 2007 and continuing in 2008 and 2009, the world economy suddenly and precipitously tanked. Although most citizens do not know this, the United States very quickly ceased to be the economic leader of the world. Most Americans, however, know their economic losses are enormous. China, India and all Asia are saying American free enterprise did not work, so some form of Asian free enterprise should be used. The Chinese form?

A new President was elected largely on "the need for change." The federal government stepped in with huge bailouts.

At least 10 percent of Americans lost their jobs and many, many are still out of work and will continue to be so while thousands of others are taking lesser paying jobs.

How does this impact our spiritual life? This economic collapse is a test of our current way of living, our everyday habits and customs. The questions are these: Are we "economic people" more than we are "spiritual people"? Are we serving God or mammon more? Are we spending too much on things we want, but do not need? Are we saving for a rainy day? Are we too used to the finer things of life? Can we cut down our credit card debt? Can we make our mortgage payments?

This is an eight-part examination of the above questions that includes suggestions on how we can live a richer Christian spiritual life in the midst of economic scarcity and perhaps even *because* of it.

Every work is dependent on other sources and this one is no exception. For the economic analysis, the author turned to those who have the best and brightest insights today. And for spiritual analysis, the author turned to ancient, modern and postmodern Christian sources.

So often, average Americans are so busy with their families and making a living that they do not take time in the day to see this bigger picture which impacts their lives mightily. The purpose of this book is to help all Americans, including the laity, priests, religious and hierarchy, to realize the magnitude of how times have changed and the opportunity and urgency this presents to make appropriate adjustments in our way of life, both spiritual and temporal.

When the Japanese bombed Pearl Harbor on December 7, 1941, the American people were jolted into the realization that they needed to think differently, act differently and pray differently, lest our way of life simply be trampled on by the totalitarian powers of the world. Everything changed.

Before that, when the Great Depression descended upon the world, all Americans realized that they had to change and learn survival strategies and ways to prosper.

Similarly, the purpose of this book is for everyone to realize the magnitude of the world economic collapse and the opportunity it presents us to change just about everything. It is that big. It is that important.

It needs to impact our Church. It needs to impact our practices. It needs to impact our purchasing. It needs to impact our praying. It needs to impact our planning. It needs to impact our pursuit of happiness.

And what about 2010? A *Commonweal* article in January 2011 said it best: "Wall Street is back, but what about the rest of us?" Yes, Wall Street had a strong comeback in 2010. The biggest New York banks have billions of dollars of year-end bonuses now. "But what about the rest of us?"

I Want It All.
I Want It Now.

Do you remember the Chase Bank commercial which ran over and over again in 2007: "I want it all. I want it now."

Few of us, in that year, realized how dangerous this was. Our economic leaders surely did not tell us. Our politicians surely did not warn us. And our preachers surely did not pay much attention to it.

Our world has changed

Every year, previously, our homes increased in value. And every year, we seemed to want more goods and services and we came to expect more goods and services. Our salaries continued to rise. Our economy continued to flourish. We were all encouraged to spend, spend, spend with credit easily available.

It was a very seductive time. Most people vaguely knew they were spending too much but, like an adolescent who has three traffic tickets unpaid with failure to appear in court and a warrant out for his arrest, they felt that if they did not pay attention to it, it just might go away.

Our political, economic, and spiritual leaders really did fail us in this regard, fail us very badly. And when the collapse came in 2007, 2008, and 2009, it came with a vengeance, as we shall see very shortly. The world has changed and it has changed for all of us. We are no longer free to borrow, borrow, borrow. Credit is tight. We are no longer free to rack up huge bills on our credit cards. We are no longer free to spend, spend, spend. Many are out of work, up to 10 percent of the work force. The world will not be the same as it was just a few years ago.

We are now being told, and rightly so, about something we forgot long ago, namely, that thrift is important. Our leaders and we, too, were engaging in what we now see in hindsight as selfishness and overspending which are wrong, and what we need is to restrain ourselves and rediscover thrift and moderation.

It was St. Paul who said: I learned to live in abundance and I have learned to live with scarcity. If the world has changed, what do we do? You and I cannot change the world. We cannot change the economy. But we can change ourselves. Yes, there are ways we can change ourselves with the grace of God. And then the world might change.

Looking back, it is easy to see that we forgot to restrain ourselves, we forgot moderation and we forgot self-discipline. "I want it all...I want it now." We sort of thought that would be just fine. We were blindsided. We wanted to be free to spend as we liked. We wanted to be free from some of the moral restraints of the past (thrift, hard work, self-sacrifice, discipline).

The mantra: freedom from restraints

But we were not the only ones who forgot. Our political and economic leaders shamelessly abandoned traditional moral restraints of fiscal responsibility. In the simplest of terms, they abandoned the Golden Rule. A little fudging, a little lying, a little cheating, a little stealing would not be so bad. We will see in a later chapter that there is a basic rule of anthropology: Leaders gain and maintain power, not only by money but by making sure their view dominates and prevails. We were lower on the economic ladder and, when our leaders kept assuring us that everything was just fine, their views prevailed. We believed them. We shall see how they themselves now admit, in their best moments, making the grossest of errors.

Let us try to put this in perspective. Do you remember when we were adolescents? What we wanted more than anything else was to be free from restraints. Nobody policing us. How many times did we say to ourselves: No one is going to tell me what to do? In our adolescent fantasy world at the time we believed we could perhaps lie a little, cheat a little, steal a little and get away with it. Cheating in school was commonplace. Cheating in sports was commonplace. Lying to our girl-friends or boyfriends was commonplace and petty steal-ing was universally visible, as any shopkeeper would tell us. It came as a shocking realization that sometimes we got caught lying. But we did not repent. Many of us just lied more to cover it up. It came also as a shocking real-ization that if we cheated in school we did not always get caught, but some day it might catch up with us and it did for many. And we remember those who continued to steal, sooner or later, almost always got caught.

And yet, as adolescents, many continued to lie, cheat and steal. And many adolescents, and those older, con-tinued to prolong their immaturity by embracing free-dom from sexual restraints. Following the mass media, there are those who continued to engage in sex without feeling, and not just adolescents, boys ripping off girls, girls ripping off boys, pornography and all other manner of perversity. The result was often depression, loneliness, and alienation. Here at Boys Town, we see this with the kids who come to us. They are not happy when we insist freedom without moral restraints is hurtful.

It is very curious for this author to reflect on how this mantra of freedom from restraints, so prevalent in adolescence, moved into the political and economic realm of adulthood in financial matters. Here it simply means that, slowly but surely, the profit motive was allowed to be less restrained by any sense of justice or fairness, by government regulations, or by our consciences. Slowly it caught us off guard. We did not think on it much.

Most adults know instinctively that if we do not put taboos on lying, cheating and stealing that they will grow and flourish. But somehow in the economic sector, our leaders began to let the market (freedom from restraint) prevail and the heck with everything else. "Free markets must be totally free", was their mantra. What mattered was profit. It did not matter if you fudged a bit or cheated a bit or even a lot. Harbingers were Enron where there was a massive corporate network of enriching those at the top and lying to those below. There was the collapse of World Com. But everyone thought these were an aberration. Then there was the collapse of Arthur Anderson, and people began to say perhaps this is not an aberration.

This became a very malignant form of American capitalism. It was not a healthy form of free enterprise which is based on justice, fairness, a free exchange of goods, private property and a condemnation of greed and malice. Healthy free enterprise is good in unleashing human creativity in the economic sector. The positive role of business is helpful when combined with justice and caring.

The triumph of self-interest

But what began to emerge, as we shall see in later chapters, was a huge global economy where economic leaders and government regulators did not put viable limits on the economic sector in terms of justice and fairness. They started to believe: "Self-interest will triumph." They were like adolescents, thinking freedom from restraint was a positive stance. They began to believe it just as adolescents did. At the top of the economic ladder, at the bottom and sometimes in the middle, greed, lying, cheating and even self-deception were allowed to flourish without most of us noticing it. Some (not us of course) call it "making the fast buck."

But lest we be too hard on everyone, it is good to remember that basic principle of anthropology, namely: Elites gain and maintain power, not only by having money but by also making sure their view dominates and prevails. The elites claimed, as they always have, superior intelligence, superior wisdom and the power to enforce silence on anyone who disagreed. It has always been difficult to tell truth to power. So few, if any, did.

If we did not have police pursuing robbers, there would be more robberies. If we did not have governmental restraints in financial areas, we would have more lying and cheating. And that is what happened. It all began with the insistence that we should have fewer banking regulations, more self-regulation.

Who was one of the chief proponents of this? Alan Greenspan and many others like him. Greenspan for two decades (1987-2006) was Chairman of the Federal Reserve with great influence on Congress, the White House and others in promoting deregulation of financial markets. He would say that markets worked best when left alone (freedom from restraint). Many nodded their heads in agreement. That sounded great to a lot of people. No mention of justice, fairness or regulation by others. Greenspan argued that government intervention was a problem, not a solution. Many nodded their heads in agreement to this, too. He always advocated for less regulation and called it voluntary oversight. That is like telling the night manager at McDonald's that when he closes and counts the cash drawer, no one else will re-count it. It will all be on the honor system with no further checking. No business owner, in his right mind, would allow that. But that is the beginning of what we did in banking. "Let us use the honor system." When the honor system is used in schools, it is the teachers who have the honor and the students who have the system. It is important to remember that, even in banking. This is not a universal indictment of bankers. But it is an indictment of some.

Where did the ideas come from behind this lessening of regulation and embrace of voluntary oversight? In the 1950s, Alan Greenspan joined the inner circle of Ayn Rand who believed that self-absorption, not self-donation, was the answer and not the problem. He joined her inner circle in the 1950s. She praised those who pursue their own advantage regardless of others as long as it was not done by force or fraud. She said: "You have no responsibility to others except through self-restraint and self-interest." She said: "Individual happiness is the ultimate good." In the 1950s, Alan Greenspan believed that and later put it into practice as Chairman of the Federal Reserve. He said it this way: "There should be less government regulation, there should be self-regulation guided by the self-interested." He said that self-interest (code word for selfishness) would stop people from being unjust, unfair and greedy. How foolish that was. He said that was the way to great freedom and great prosperity. He followed Ayn Rand's book written in 1964 called *The Virtue of Selfishness.*

On October 23, 2008, Alan Greenspan appeared shame-faced before the Government Oversight and Reform Committee of the U.S. House of Representatives. The economy was in shambles. He admitted there was "a flaw" in his beliefs about self-interest and market forces. He said:

> "Those of us who have looked to the self-interest of leading institutions to protect shareholder equity, myself included, are in a state of shocked disbelief."

Too many people believed that and yet did not intend to hurt others. Subtle, yes, but greed nonetheless and no one was reminding us of that. It was nothing more than greed. Instead of saying "I want it all," if we are honest and conscientious, we should be saying "I would like to have my fair share and we need to make sure others have their fair share, too, including the poor." Instead of saying "I want it now," we should be saying "I need to save. I need to discipline myself. I have to think of others and be fair with them."

Too many people think of our economic system as a sophisticated money-driven matrix "creating" wealth, driving progress in production and technology. But what if it only does that for a few people of the world while many, many, many others do not get a share and are in abject poverty as they are in Third World countries? Is that fair? Is that good? No.

Here in our country it was this greedy self-interest (not intending to hurt others) that propelled our largest banks to successfully negotiate a bill in Congress in 1983 that would, to all extents and purposes, bypass the restrictions of how much interest credit card companies could charge. It was usually pegged at 17 or 18 percent. The law in 1983 was changed to say that if a bank or credit card company had a headquarters in a state where there were no restrictions, such as South Dakota, then the credit card company could allow the "no restriction on interest" rule throughout the United States. This was in the banking industry's own self-interest.

Many of us received two or three monthly solicitations for credit cards. How many did you get in the mail in 2008? There was a Boys Town alumnus who came to me with nineteen credit cards and $38,000 in credit debt on them, and there was no way he could pay. I helped, through Credit Advisors, to consolidate his debts, but then found out he had received and accepted three more credit cards in the following two months. When I chided him for it, he said: "What could I do? They made these offers in the mail and I simply accepted them and they sent me a credit card." Credit card debt has tripled with many people having, up until now, little thought of paying it off.

One of our recent high school graduates who is going to college said he did not qualify for a Stafford loan but did receive a private student loan from a bank. I asked him if he intended to pay it back. He said: "Why would I have to pay it back? I think it is like a Pell grant." By the way, so many kids say that a Pell grant at certain colleges is what they call "free money." The money comes to you. You do not have to spend it on school and there is no need to repay it. All you have to do is be enrolled in school the day you receive it. This all seems to be very selfish, very unfair, and very unjust.

Our biggest moral threat is financial

You would not be surprised to hear me say that our most pressing moral threat in the United States is not sexual, but financial. It will destroy our lives. The sexual moral threat is huge. The financial moral threat is even greater, if that is possible.

Several years ago a variety of church leaders, with general concerns for the poor, argued that "redlining" is immoral. (Redlining is the refusal to lend money or extend credit to those living in certain disadvantaged areas of cities.) They were correct. They also argued that credit should be available to the poor. This was also a good idea. In their enthusiasm, they forgot to mention that it should not be given to people who cannot pay it back. They meant we should make credit available to the poor so they do not have to go to loan sharks. Going to loan sharks is a bad idea. Making credit available is a good idea as long as it does not trick the poor into taking out loans they cannot pay back! That is fraud. Politicians picked up on the good idea, but it mutated very quickly into a big mess. Many of the poor cannot pay back their loans. Politicians and churchmen forgot that a noble goal is worthless if not implemented properly. The end does not justify the means. Inducing the poor to take out a mortgage that you know will fail is immoral!

I sat down at a table for lunch the other day with new employees. One, very energetic, middle-age person said she was so happy to be at Boys Town. I asked her why she left the mortgage company she had been working for and she said: "I left because I just got tired of falsifying loan applications by using someone else's salary stubs."

In the next chapter, I will look at how we went from a nation of savers, namely, a thrift culture to a nation of debt ridden slouches. That Chase ad pretty well sums it up. "I want it all. I want it now." Another good example is the television show "Flip This House" where people bought and sold homes, not to live in them but to make a quick killing in the rapidly rising housing market.

A hard-working young Boys Town alum told me the story of going to buy a used car. He had only enough credit for a $7,000 loan and picked a car with an appropriate price tag. The salesman showed him a $12,000 car, which the boy liked a lot, but said he could only afford a $7,000 loan. The salesman said: "That's doesn't matter. We will use someone else's salary records when we submit the loan application." "I want it all...I want it now."

William Donaldson was head of the Federal Trade Commission when he said we needed more financial restraints. He was told no, and he quit. Good for him. But nobody listened. This financial crisis was brought to us by some of the best and brightest in the country. And some of them are saying they did not know what they were doing. My response is: You instinctively knew that as financial elites you gain and maintain power, not only by money but by making sure your view dominated and prevailed. That is irresponsible on your part. You tried to live with no intention to hurt others, but also with no deep sense of responsibility, no moral restraints. In a spring 2010 Congressional hearing with Goldman executives, there surfaced a top trader's 2007 e-mail that joked about enticing unsuspecting "widows and orphans" to invest in the imploding housing market. He also laughed about the subprime borrowers who were about to go under. Succors! As John J. Dijulio Jr. points out, "the only mistakes" to which these witnesses would admit were analytical, not ethical.

I tell our kids at Boys Town they cannot live a life without restraint, without concern for others, without a sense of justice, without a sense of fairness, and that selfishness and greed are sinful. Our political leaders knew that or should have known that, but they followed the financial crowd. So did many of our church leaders, pastors, and even bishops. The question they asked was: What's everybody else doing? The result was we are all suffering. Sometime ago, I was in New York and made remarks such as this and the chairman of a very large American company came up to me and said I was making people fearful by saying these things. I told him he had made people fearful by lack of restraints other than self-interest and he should reflect on that reality. Needless to say, we did not have any further conversation.

"I want it all. I want it now." That commercial reminds me of some of our boys and girls who come from very, very poor families and who complain to me: Why can't we buy brand name foods such as Del Monte? Why do we have to buy store brands? They do not know that the same company makes both. But they have been told that even though you are poor you should still be able to buy the costliest brand names. I mentioned this one day at dinner with some very, very wealthy people. One of them said: "This just goes to show you, Father Peter, that the poor have very good taste and a demand for quality." My response: "This just goes to show you that someone taught even the poor to want it all and to want it now."

Getting up this morning, it dawned on me that you and I and all citizens...on the basis of the mother of all bailouts given by the government to banks, to AIG, to General Motors and so many others...are owners of all kinds of debt we did not ask for or agree to. It is called the national debt. In fact, we American citizens are the largest holders of bad debt, perhaps in the world.

In conclusion, we need to discipline ourselves and we need to shed ourselves of the conviction that we should be free from all restraints. We need to help our brothers and sisters. We need to practice self-discipline. We have to start with very small things in denying ourselves. We need to pray every night: Lord, make me a more disciplined person. Make me more unselfish.

Perhaps, like Alan Greenspan, many of us trusted those in important positions in government, banking and industry to be people of character and virtue. Some were, but too many were not.

CHAPTER TWO

The Thrift Culture vs. the 'I Want It All' Culture

Being born in the heart of the Depression (1934) and raised during World War II, I lived in a family that was part of the thrift culture. We were surrounded by thrift institutions and practices that in spirit went all the way back to Ben Franklin.

The thrift culture

As children, we all had very small savings accounts. I remember putting in eleven cents a month. My grandmother would take the streetcar downtown (cost: five cents) each month to pay her gas bill, electric bill, and telephone bill and deposit $2 in the Conservative Savings and Loan Association. She thus saved the expense of four three-cent stamps and enjoyed the outing.

In World War II, my brothers and I would buy five-cent U. S. savings stamps at the grocery store and put them in a booklet until we had $18 which would buy us a $25 war bond.

Everybody we knew saved in this way through credit unions, building and loan associations, and other non-profit banking places. We were what were called "small savers." In the fall, parents bought Christmas gifts on layaway plans. We were taught that saving for a rainy day was important. You would need money for high school and for college. When my parents came to buy a house, they needed a down payment of at least $1,000 saved for their first house which cost $5,000. They had to go to the bank and show their credit worthiness. There were limits set by the government on the interest and fees the bank could charge. My brothers and I studied mightily so we could get into a private prep school where the tuition was $76.50 per semester. You could make that much money if you had a paper route and saved.

We knew there were other shady ways of obtaining money. The pawn shops were across the river, together with the peep shows and skid row. We knew there were loan sharks and numbers games which our parents taught us were a waste of money and a financial rip off. They taught us that if you wanted to go to this good school, you had to save and pay up front. We did and felt good about it.

Yes, thrift and industry were virtues everyone needed in order to be successful. If you worked hard and were thrifty, you could make something of yourself. Our parents would never think of borrowing money to buy superfluous items. Dad would announce solemnly the Friday after Thanksgiving: Santa this year can afford $2.50 per child. We were sure envious of kids who had shiny new bicycles, but we knew not to ask for one as a Christmas present because our parents could not afford them and it would hurt them if we asked.

I remember my mother crying one Friday night at dinner, saying: "Boys, I am sorry all we have for dinner is pancakes. I wish there was something else." And we were not poor by any means for we were told vivid stories of families so poor that the kids took turns eating every other day (boys on Monday, Wednesday, Friday and girls on Tuesday, Thursday, Saturday with all eating on Sunday). We never thought of ourselves as anything other than middle class in hard times. And we knew that thrift and hard work were the keys to a brighter future. Greed was clearly a bad thing. Early on, I learned this prayer:

> Dear Lord,
> "Do not let me be too poor
> Or too rich.
> Give me just what I need.
> If I have too much
> I might forget you.

If I don't have enough
I might steal."
(Proverbs 30 8-9)

The coming of affluence

What happened to all of that? Well, after World War II, during which great sacrifices were made by so many Americans, a feeling of entitlement entered the minds and hearts of most Americans. The returning soldiers often said they had sacrificed so much they were entitled to a little bigger house, a little nicer car, and a little better vacation not spent at home. And the GI bill gave them a better education. Who could deny them that? Credit cards began to appear and at first they were not used by most people for credit as much as they were used in lieu of cash, and that's how they were advertised. Slowly, but surely, they became instruments of heavy debt with minimum payments required. Usury laws prohibited predatory interest rates and, in some ways, that encouraged spending and building up debt. Through a variety of influences we were slowly, but surely, becoming an affluent society.

What is affluence? Professor Peter Danner of Marquette University put it this way: affluence is a subtle change from a state of *wanting* more salary, more goods and more services to *expecting* more money, more goods and more services. We began to *expect* that this would continue on and on and so we were willing to move away from what is called a thrift culture. In a thrift culture, you save until you can afford to buy something. You work very hard and, although you want more goods and services, you do not buy them until you can afford them. But the post-World War II boom led Americans to change their expectations. Thrift began to recede more and more. We began to buy more and more on credit. Credit cards became easier to obtain and then loans became easier and easier to obtain because less collateral was needed. Then came signature loans.

I remember clearly in 1960 arriving home from Europe after six years of study there. I was a newly ordained priest making $75 a month and I applied for a Phillips 66 credit card. On the application, I stated honestly my income was $75 a month. (Priests were paid a pittance!) Well, of course, I was denied a credit card. So I changed the $75 on a new application to $750 and immediately a card was issued to me. Nobody cared to check. That was way back in 1960. By 1970, people were sending all of us offers of credit cards in the mail. By 1980 and 1990, this became much more frequent. People were piling up credit card debt and fewer and fewer people even thought of delaying purchases until they could afford it. Chase Bank had not yet started its ads: "I want it all. I want it now." But that is what was happening. We had now become affluent and debt-ridden. Candidates for president usually ask the voters: Are you better off (financially) today than you were four years ago?

Again, affluence doesn't simply mean *wanting* more salary, more goods and more services. It means *expecting* more salary, more goods and more services. The difference is startling. In Africa, for example, everyone would like to have a higher standard of living, but they do not expect it. Here in America, we expected to be making more every year, to be buying bigger and better things. Until, of course, the current economic collapse occurred.

It now is clear that we were borrowing far beyond our means. We were no longer a thrift culture, but a debt culture, an "I want it all" culture. On the horizon came subprime credit card issuers. In times past, payday lenders were in the seedy part of town. So were rent-to-own merchants. Now payday lenders, rent-to-own merchants, auto title lenders, check cashing outlets all began to appear in the new strip malls right next to the suburbs. Have you noticed the pawn shops that sprang up in the better parts of town?

And even more than that, the government jumped into the anti-thrift business by creating state-owned and operated lotteries. Before 1964, not one government-sponsored lottery existed in the United States. Today, almost every state has one. It is interesting to look at who are the most loyal customers of state-run lotteries. It is the low- and moderate-income families that, somehow

28

or other, hope to win big. So instead of saving $5 a week at a credit union, they buy five lottery tickets as a way to fantasize about instant wealth. A very poorly dressed fellow standing in front of me in the grocery store pulled out a $20 bill and spent it all on lottery tickets. If he put that $20 every week into a savings account, by year end he would have $1,040. And, of course, we forgot to mention casino gambling which previously was allowed only in Las Vegas and Atlantic City. In days gone by, those who pawned their wedding rings or gambled away their family savings or borrowed from loan sharks were viewed as destroying family life. Now they are often seen as desperately trying to hold things together.

In 2008, the Institute for American Values published a report from the Commission on Thrift, pointing out that formerly thrifty Americans in the moderate and lower economic brackets have now become habitual debtors. This is a major shift, a tragic one because it puts enormous economic pressures on families. And at the same time, the report noted there was an upper tier of richer Americans who were investing and building wealth through pro-thrift institutions. The lower tier had been serviced by anti-thrift institutions that "provide multiple ways and means for lower earning Americans to forgo savings, borrow at predatory interest rates and fall into a debt trap."

And that was all before the economic collapse. Members of what the Commission on Thrift called the lottery class (I call it the "I want it all" class) were not motivated to put aside extra dollars. They were motivated often to forgo some of their tax refund dollars in exchange for instant cash from H & R Block.

It is good to remember that a century ago in the early 1900s, (history calls this the Progressive Era) anti-thrift agencies were ripping off many hard working Americans, taking their dollars and dreams. They were "chattel lenders" or "salary lenders." But most people in those days knew them as loan sharks. The Commission on Thrift points to one writer who says that in New York City alone, one hundred years ago, three out of every ten workers owed money to loan sharks. The noble response to loan sharks was a national campaign among honest businessmen and politicians to drive them out of business. It worked. Journalists wrote exposés of their corrupt practices. They were called muckraking articles. And legislation was passed to encourage credit unions, thrift agencies of all kinds. That is all mostly gone now.

This is not to say that all borrowing is a bad thing, but it is to say that access to credit, on one hand, helps a young family to grow and to develop, to start businesses, to boost job prospects. But, on the other hand, it can also promote mounting debt, even staggering debt which slams the door on the future. The whole credit union movement had as a motive to engage in thrift and enable savers to take out low-cost loans as an alternative to pawn shops.

In our day, a pinched wage earner has more places to turn to get fast money. More than one billion credit cards are in the wallets of Americans. There is hardly one of us who has not paid late fees or been charged for missed payments on credit cards. In 2006, late fees and missed payments were at $17.1 billion in fees. And for unexpected expenses such as house repairs or car repairs or medical emergencies, there is no nest egg at the credit union, but there is a credit card.

Around 1960, banks and other institutions issuing credit cards or bank cards offered fixed interest rates to credit-worthy people. Usury laws in most states put a 12 – 14 percent cap on the interest that could be charged on credit card balances. Remember what we said above, in 1978 the Supreme Court ruled that banks could get around the usury laws by charging interest rates allowed in their own home state rather than in the consumer's home state. So if you moved your credit card operation to South Dakota, you could set whatever interest rates you wanted. Then other states responded out of fear of losing banking industry to states like South Dakota and lifted their own caps.

Now credit card folks really did build a financial model for getting people to move from thrift (healthy fear of debt) with its social stigma for people always in debt to "it is OKAY to have a heavy debt load." Barbara Defoe Whitehead says it this way: "The credit card industry was the great innovator in how to get people into debt and keep them there." Consumers now bought more than they could afford and were happy doing so. People's self-image changed from being stogy old saviors like Ben Franklin into "shop till you drop" buyers.

The credit card people (once they achieved the magic of having folks want it all) realized they could make a lot more profit if instead of issuing short term credit to financially solvent customers, they extended long term credit to financially shaky customers. Card companies made minimum payments as low as possible and encouraged card holders to only pay the minimum. This is unsavory!

And, of course, then they discovered the student market. These were kids in college who were told to buy right now what they wanted and put it on their credit cards. The credit card companies counted on their parents to bail them out and oftentimes they did. The credit card folks also demolished the traditional banking relationship between lender and borrower. Today, for example, I have three credit cards and on only one of them do I have a depository account. The result of all this is that many, many Americans are now dependent on expensive credit.

And don't forget what we call the "democratization" of credit. It started as a good idea way back in the early 1900s when poor immigrants needed access to small loans (unsecured consumer loans). The banks at the time began issuing them (with regulators allowing higher interest rates so they could make a profit, but lower rates than the loan sharks). Credit unions were another good facet of democratization of credit. So were layaway plans and insurance.

There was now a difference between good debt and bad debt. It's a noble motive in helping the poor avoid loan sharks but, in many cases, it didn't turn out to be so noble. The best example is the subprime lending market where the poor ended up with more debt than they could ever pay off. Spending also was based on impulse buying. A poor young couple the other day told me they ran up $60 of credit card debt in two weeks at McDonald's, Burger King and Wendy's. But, despite these widespread abuses, democratization of credit still is a good idea if used wisely. The noble end does not justify immoral means! As seen above, it is immoral to talk the poor into taking out a mortgage or loan you know they cannot or won't repay.

The great recession

And now we have been in a very severe recession with millions and millions of Americans laid off, with our homes worth far less than they were before and with many, even in the culture of wealth, experiencing a decline of 30 to 40 percent in their 401(k)s, profit-sharing plans, Keogh plans, deferred income compensation plans, and retirement savings plans. Whether we like it or not, it's time to take seriously the task of rediscovering thrift.

Yes, we are in tough financial times and these tough times are calling into question our current way of living. With forty-three out of fifty states now facing huge budget deficits in 2011, our way of living is being even more challenged now. When things get tough, it is time to go back to the basics of thrift – only spend when you have saved up for the purchase. There are bright spots in economic hard times and we need to focus on them. One great benefit of tough times is we are much more structurally motivated to help one another. Let's take examples from the family. In these times, it is better to limit going out to eat and it is much better to have family meals. That is a plus. In these times, it is structurally better to live at home. And to do so, we have to try harder to get along with each other, to treat each other as brothers and sisters. In these times, it is much better to pay down our credit card balances. We learn to get along with less – entertainment, excursions, clothes, etc.

It is a good time to sit down with your children and explain in simple honest terms, without panic, that the family has to reduce spending and that we can do it by becoming closer to one another, helping one another more, relying more on our faith.

And we can explain to our children that it would be good for them not to ask for as many expensive gifts as they have in the past. We can even suggest they help with their tuition. And if they see us, their parents, doing without certain luxuries we are accustomed to, they will be inspired by our role modeling.

There are three basic themes we are suggesting you consider adopting as a family.

The first theme is this: **If you learn to live within your means, you will learn to live with less.** And if you live with less, you will be far happier.

The second theme is that **self-donation is much more important than self-absorption.** Helping others is much more important than being selfish. Caring for one another, helping each other is much more important than looking out for yourself. At the last judgment as described in Matthew 25, the questions that will be asked of you are all about self-donation. I was hungry and you gave me nothing to eat. I was thirsty and you gave me nothing to drink.

The third theme is that **who you are is much more important than what you have.** You are first and foremost a child of God, a member of a family. You are one of God's people, together with others, called and sent to bring the Good News.

It is a great time to discover and nourish family life, togetherness, caring, and sharing. It is time to return to Ben Franklin's ideas of economic freedom. Economic freedom is freedom from the worry of mounting bills and no way to pay them off. Immigrants quickly bought his idea of frugality and industry, namely, working hard, saving wisely and spending modestly so as to achieve a state of well being liberated from the worries, burdens and anxieties that so filled the lives of the very poor in his time, and the overly debt ridden in our time. We have to feel good about saving and bad about over-spending.

Postscript: Please go to the Web site of the Institute for American Values and see "A Report to the Nation from the Commission on Thrift." It is great reading!

CHAPTER THREE

A Christian View of Scarcity and Plenty

Even before the economic downturn many Americans sensed something wrong with our consumer society. They often felt a sense of spiritual unease knowing, as they did, they were consuming too many of the world's resources and sharing too little with those less fortunate. They were often assured "not to worry."

Voices before the economic collapse

When writers addressed these concerns, before the economic collapse, few paid attention. See, for example, Vincent Miller, *Consuming Religion* (2005); Thomas Frank, *One Market under God* (2000); David Crocher and Toby Linden, *Ethics of Consumption* (1998); William Schweiker and Charles Mathewes, eds., *Having Property and Possession in Religious and Social Life* (2004).

Other writers turned to Karl Marx's withering critique of capitalism. Granted, he was writing of the early industrialization of 19th Century Europe. Yet, despite the ultimate failure of his program, he had some useful, critical insights about the false consciousness of the wealthy vis-à-vis the poor. His moral outrage at the exploitation of workers struck a sympathetic cord in the hearts of some. But his central notion of class struggle taught too many people to hate the rich. No just society can be built on hatred. John Francis Kavanaugh in *Following Christ in a Consumer Society* (1982) used a Marxist critique to help focus on the power of the gospel to transform the lives of consumers. Unfortunately, his use of a Marxist critique was a turnoff to many so they missed the point of Kavanaugh's, otherwise, excellent advice on how to follow Christ in a consumer society.

Dorothy Day, once a dedicated Marxist who became a Christian, wrote in her autobiography, *The Long Loneliness* (1952): "If I could have felt that Communism was the answer to my desire for a cause, a motive, a way to live in, I would have remained as I was. But I felt that only faith in Christ could give the answer. The Sermon on the Mount answered all the questions as to how to love God and one's neighbor."

Similarly, others looked for ways to address a consumer society in the writings of humanistic psychologists.

For example, Abraham Maslow was convinced that humanistic psychology was a perfect replacement for the materialism of the age. Many Christians embraced Maslow's teaching without realizing he wanted humanistic psychology to also replace not just materialism but also even ecclesial institutions such as the Catholic Church. He writes in his diary of a talk he gave to nuns in 1962 at Sacred Heart College in Newton, Massachusetts. "They shouldn't applaud me. They should attack me. If they were fully aware of what I was doing, they would."

Or take, for example, Carl Rogers who started the human potential movement. In 1960 he published *On Becoming a Person*, popularizing the idea that to become a person, one has to find the "real me" and get rid of all the false me's that socialization, including materialism, creates. Very unfortunately, Rogers set aside the whole marvelous Christian tradition on scarcity and plenty. His work did not have the impact he thought it would, namely, a liberating impact. Sometimes it made simply a narcissistic impact. Too often the Christian message at the time of Vatican II was cast aside unjustly because our message was presented in a somewhat outdated unattractive wrapping and the wrapping was confused with the gift.

After the economic collapse

Now let us turn to the power and glory of the Lord's way to deal with material goods in times of scarcity.

The economic downturn has touched the lives of countless Americans. As I write this, there are millions of American workers who have lost their jobs. Countless retired persons have seen the funds they were counting on shrink by 30 or 40 or 50 percent. Some have recouped losses, but not enough. Many are badly shaken. Here at Boys Town, our graduates of 2009 and 2010 need $12-an-hour jobs to make ends meet. And about the only ones available are $10-an-hour temp services.

On a different level, a friend of mine was let go by downsizing, losing his $60,000 a year job. He has a wife who is a homemaker and two children, ages 10 and 16. He is in a state of shock. He is feeling helpless and he is just plain depressed. You can see the darkness descending on his life. Yes, his family right now is a dark place. There is lots of bitterness. There is lots of sadness. There is a feeling of being betrayed.

A 40-year-old lady delivered flowers from a local florist to us at Dowd Chapel yesterday. And I said: "I have never seen you before." She told me she had lost her job so she has to deliver flowers two days a week. "That way I will get a little money." Then she shook her head and said, "Life just isn't fair." That is true, but it is not much of a consolation. She, too, is complaining, perhaps reasonably. She seemed close to hopelessness, as she lamented: "I drive to the next place, deliver a lousy flower and then another lousy flower at the next place and get a lousy, measly salary." She is close to losing hope.

The flower lady and my friend already realize that in some ways their lives were helped greatly by abundance. They had fun going out to dinner, they had fun buying a nice new car, they had fun going on vacations, they had fun making happy memories. They thought it would never end. But when it did, the time had come to let Christian faith do its own marvelous work. That marvelous work begins with the realization that this dark cloud has a silver lining. It is a wake-up call.

In a sense, it almost forces them to realize that in some ways their lives have been impoverished by abundance in comparison with many years ago when they were less affluent. How many times have you said to yourself as you walk through your home early in the morning before anyone is up that you have more of this world's goods, but are not any happier? How many times have you said to yourself that your children have too much and are getting selfish? They do not know how to sacrifice. How many times have you wished they could learn to sacrifice? How many times have you thought to yourself that economic abundance has not brought you peace of mind, but has rather brought you pernicious debts rising faster than your income? That is a wake-up call.

In other words, we realize that affluence has done wonderful things, but in the same breath it has created insecurity in the sense that the more income we have the more wants we have. It has created a much more complex, hectic life. It has created a different kind of insecurity, that all of us complain we are always in a hurry, always in a rat race and always on the treadmill. We complain we do not have enough time to read, we do not have enough time to pray, and we do not have enough wisdom or love or friendship. Despite all the goodness of God's material creation, we know our affluence has also eroded parental authority in our families. We know that our kids' culture is too often a culture of money. It is what I call erosion by affluence. Rain is good for the crops, but if it rains too much or too hard there is erosion on the land.

It is now time to talk about the great spiritual gifts our Christian faith gives us that enable us to find happiness in good times and in bad, "for richer, for poorer." The gift of faith is a pearl of great price. Let us go slowly here. Something very important, but subtle, gradually befalls us when we arise to the level of affluence that we had before the economic collapse. Notice how material possessions and economic well being make us towering promises which they cannot keep, promises that riches will bring us happiness and satisfaction and self-fulfillment. Riches cannot possibly do that.

Material emptiness

Why? Because at the heart of all these material possessions, material gains, and material success is the kind of emptiness of material things. *Our Christian tradition calls it material emptiness or ontological poverty.* It is not that material things are bad. They are not. They are God's good creation. They are to be enjoyed. It is rather that material things and economic well being can satisfy certain hungers, but they can never satisfy the deepest hungers of the human spirit. "Man does not live on bread alone." There is a longing in the depths of each of our hearts which can never be satisfied by material goods or by a higher standard of living. St. Augustine said it well: "Our souls were made for thee, O God, and they will not rest until they rest in thee." To rest in material goods or to embrace them too much brings the trivialization of life. Too many riches cannot bring about a rich life.

Christians through the centuries have asked what the remedy is for this emptiness at the heart of material things. And the answer through the Centuries has been this: Only the *evangelical spirit of poverty* found in the gospels and in Jesus' teaching can fill the material emptiness or ontological poverty. Yes, the evangelical spirit of poverty alone can bring meaning to the frustration that material goods generate. It alone can bring deep enjoyment of the good things in life. The gospel's spirit of poverty alone can answer the question so often expressed by us: I have so much more than my grandparents or parents, but what good has it done me? What good has it done anyone else? It is not that material goods are bad. It is rather that they are pitched to us by a marketing world that entices and tempts us. It is a way to satisfy the artificial wants created by our culture. "If I only had a new car or a better home or a bigger salary, then I would really be happy." And yet we know deep down that is not true, that after a few days our new car doesn't bring us promised happiness and now we want something else. Yes, material goods generate more wants, more wants, more wants. Christian authors, such as Professor Peter Danner, have often put it this way: Affluence creates scarcity and that brings emptiness.

Affluence tempts us to believe if we love our children, we will give them the best, namely, more material things. But only materialism makes us believe that is the best. The best is really calling them to loving God and our neighbor. The best is calling them to a life of virtue and moral greatness.

With the economic downturn, almost all of us realize that we are too far in debt and the more we have the more we spend, the more we worry and the deeper the debt piles up. We need the spirit of poverty to fill this emptiness.

Yes, we get hooked on material goods. But they bring us less freedom, not more. Remember the ad for Chase Bank: "I want it all. I want it now."

And if I want it now and want it all, I just may be tempted to buy too much on credit, to forget to save for rainy days. After all, only suckers do those things. And this attitude doesn't just involve material goods. It spills over to other areas of our lives. "What happens in Vegas stays in Vegas." Only suckers believe otherwise. So we are tempted to cheat on other things, in marriage, in family, in business, in pleasure.

And now we come to a very hard saying. If you have been reading this so far, you found me saying there are sound, honest businessmen and women, but there are also those who are greedy, villains and rogues, both in government and in business. But that is not the whole problem. You and I did not create the subprime mortgage crisis. But you and I may fall into the trap of believing everything will be okay once blame is fixed and the villains exposed. But there is a problem in our heart, yours and mine, a big problem, namely, a lack of a gospel spirit of poverty.

If we look into the scriptures, we will see certain ideas about poverty jump out at us. In the Old Testament in early Israel, the journey to the Promised Land by the nomadic Hebrew people found all of them being, more or less, equally poor. On coming into the Promised Land

and especially when Saul became king and other kings followed, there was an increase of wealth among the upper class and dire poverty elsewhere. Amos, the prophet, cries out against oppression of the poor, the denial of basic dignity to them, unjust demands for debt repayment. Other prophets followed suit. The Lord does not forget the cry of the poor.

There is another theme in the Old Testament, that poverty and disaster are the result of Israel's unfaithfulness to the Lord. In the Wisdom literature, there is a middle state between excessive wealth and excessive want, a state most helpful for virtuous living. We should not have too much, lest we be tempted to rely on ourselves and not on God. And we should not have too little and be tempted to curse God. The person with this spirit of poverty is one who trusts the Lord in good times and in bad. This person furthers God's holy purposes.

Four steps in spiritual poverty

Many authors, when speaking of spiritual poverty, point to four steps that can be seen as spiritual poverty grows in our hearts to maturity. Let us look at the steps in this process.

In the first step (from Exodus to the prophets), the people of Israel are told that if they follow the covenant with their whole heart and soul, God will literally bless

Zion with material well being. This is God's promise to Israel and the promise is to the community, not to individuals. So if you are a person in the community who has more, then you have to share with those who have less. You are literally an active agent of God in bringing material well being to those who have less. Over and over, we read in the Old Testament that those who have plenty should provide special help to the orphan and the widow. Sharing your material wealth with those who have less is part of Israel's faithfulness to the covenant. Spiritual poverty is about what you do with your wealth.

In the second step, spiritual poverty is interiorized. This is during the exile. In the exile in Babylon, the children of Israel underwent real true physical poverty. What did they do with it? Some interiorized it by giving themselves to the will of God, patient in tribulation, trusting the Lord that He and His justice will someday rectify their plight.

In the third step, we see the Son of God come down from heaven seeking and preferring poverty. This adds a new dimension to the interiorization of poverty, namely, that you seek it and prefer it.

St. Francis of Assisi saw Jesus' life as a song of praise to poverty. He was born in a stable. He grew up in obscurity. He was a village carpenter of no public account and in His ministry, He took, with gratitude, whatever people gave Him...water from a Samaritan woman at

Jacob's well, a fine meal from the rich man, Zacchaeus, a donkey from a stranger to ride into Jerusalem and, finally, a burial place in someone else's tomb.

When asked what it was like to follow Him, He said: "The birds of the air have their nests, foxes have their lair, but the Son of Man has no place to lay His head."

And then there are those sayings of the Lord where Jesus warns us about how seductive wealth can be... "woe to you rich"..."woe to you who have your fill now"..."if you would be perfect, go sell what you have"..."seek first the kingdom of heaven"...prefer spiritual wealth over material wealth.

In the fourth step, we see the early Church, the apostles and their followers taking Christ's words and example and applying them to themselves. All said that the spirit of poverty...according to their circumstances...is an essential ingredient on the way to salvation. Yet remember they still kept their property. Jerusalem was unique in holding possessions in common and, even there, the surrender of private possessions was not mandatory.

They developed that marvelous idea coming from the gospels that we are not owners of the goods of this world, but only stewards. Those things have been given to us by God to use for the sake of the kingdom. We are caretakers of God's goodness. God gave us these things to use for a while as good stewards.

Wealth was for the good of all. It was a way to unite, not to divide.

In other words, what does the spirit of Christian poverty do for us? The spirit of Christian poverty asks us to "consider the lilies of the field and the birds of the air." It asks us to *trust the goodness of God* in all ways. Christian poverty asks us *to be open to the needs of others*. Dives' sin was not that he mistreated Lazarus, but that he just did not notice him or even care. In other words, our desire for wealth has to be moderated by our willingness to share. The only things we ever keep are those we give away.

In summary, spiritual poverty gives us a number of important messages. Mother Teresa pointed out that the poor of the world have a *sacramental* meaning. Here, in the poor, we encounter Christ. The poor are those with physical needs and those with spiritual needs. Spiritual poverty cautions us about too many material goods that can corrode our souls and make our commitments difficult. The widow's might is a powerful message. Genuine spiritual poverty can help us in our current economic crisis.

In other words, only the Christian spirit of poverty trusting deeply in God can calm the emptiness or restlessness that is produced in good economic times and in bad economic times. By helping others we can fill the emptiness that is at the heart of our material possessions.

In the end, let us compare this Christian spirit of poverty with two opposing views.

First, let's remember the *Christian spirit of poverty* trusts in the Lord in good times and in bad and never forgets the poor and is grateful for whatever God gives to use on our way to heaven.

In contrast to this Christian view, a *Marxist view* is that we should envy and despise those who are rich. We should pull them down. We should reduce them to poverty. We should overtax them. There should be class warfare. We should hate them.

Then there is the *secular view* that is so pervasive in our society today, namely, that money creates power. Here is what one author has to say: "Like a king, a person with money is endowed with great power. But by waving a handful of money in the air an otherwise insignificant person can command people to wait on them to satisfy their every need and will shine their shoes, clean their clothes, pour their wine, satisfy their needs and desires. A $50 bill can work magic in a restaurant, making a nonexistent table suddenly appear out of nowhere. A $100 bill can produce even more stunning results. Money clearly has a magical quality to it. It is power. It says: I can give whatever you need. Put your trust in me."

Postscript: for further study, read a good biography of St. Francis of Assisi, also John McKenzie's, *Dictionary of the Bible* under the heading poverty or riches. See also Christopher Lasch's *Culture of Narcissism* (1978). Also Jacques Ellul, *The Technological Society* (1964). An excellent book to read is Peter L. Danner's *An Ethics for the Affluent* (1980). Many ideas in this chapter come from these authors.

CHAPTER FOUR

Ethical Challenges Surrounding Wealth and Poverty

For hundreds of years, the people who lived in this country before us surrounded their lives with ethical wisdom about money, power, and sex. They tried to steer a course between puritanical suppression of pleasure on one hand (being insensitive to the good things of life), and on the other hand, wanton indulgence (coming to wallow in materialism). Remember the ad for Chase Bank: "I want it all. I want it now."

Our thoughts here focus on a middle ground between the two and the challenges that this presents. We call it the right balance between the two extremes. We call it moderation. It is the right balance that puts the brakes on the downward drag of materialism. It is the right balance that calls us to be slightly countercultural in order to go against the pleas that "everyone has it" and "everyone wants it", in other words, breaking the pattern of that kind of political correctness.

There are many excellent books written on this subject. Jane Hammerslough has written a marvelous book *Dematerializing – Taming the Power of Possessions* (2001). There is also a good anthology of ancient and modern voices raised in praise of simplicity edited by Goldian VandenBroeck entitled *Less Is More* (1996). And then there is Duane Elgin's *Voluntary Simplicity – Toward a Way of Life That Is Outwardly Simple, Inwardly Rich* (1993). All of these are very good. And even more important than these is a similar work by Peter Danner, *An Ethics for the Affluent* (1980).

Anger and arrogance

If we are to look at the basic elements of a balance between riches and poverty, we might wisely start with very visible dangers that, if unchecked, come into our lives from poverty and wealth. This will help us move toward a right balance.

All of the above authors point out that affluent Americans want too much and expect too much. This tends to become a main focus as it makes them very unhappy in times of prosperity. Perhaps unhappy is the wrong word. Perhaps the right word is that it makes them slightly uneasy, staying on the superficial level of life and avoiding the depths. There is often a kind of unconscious arrogance, almost a false consciousness. There is an emptiness in material things. It is lurking in the shadows, but it is often medicated by an extravagant lifestyle.

The challenge to those of us who have suffered financial losses is to learn how to subordinate our wants, *especially our sensual appetites (more economic goods) to higher goals.*

We want to go to Aspen, as we have always done in January, but we cannot go. Yet we notice the biggest banks, which helped precipitate the economic collapse, are planning year-end bonuses of $90 billion (January 1, 2011). We cannot go to Cape Cod for two weeks in the summer, as we have always done. But some of the super-rich are going for the whole summer. And that hurts. Or it is as simple as this, namely, we cannot go out to eat as often as we did or spend as much on entertainment. The challenge is to subordinate our wants to higher goals without frustration and without anger becoming greater and greater and greater. Our jealousy of others who have more than we and have recovered from the economic slump, sometimes taunts us.

When that happens, it is time to embrace the higher goal of family togetherness. If we open our hearts to bitterness, we will have room for nothing else. Wouldn't it be wonderful if we could have family meetings about these matters and decide what to do instead of going to Aspen? And what to do instead of going to Cape Cod? Family things! Mom and dad can take the lead here in role modeling "less conspicuous consumption." And wouldn't it be great if we join others, not in hating the super-rich but calling them (through politics, through churches and through business associations) to follow the Golden Rule?

Another important challenge is to exercise control over our appetite for gain. We told the story earlier of the man who spends $20 every week on the lottery in the hopes of winning it big. If he put the $20 in a savings account, he would have more than $1,000 each year saved. And breaking the lottery habit would control his appetite for gain. This is a kind of detachment that can be very holy. "Seek first the kingdom of heaven and all these things will be given to you besides."

There is another ethical challenge surrounding our appetite for power. With wealth comes power. A $100 bill is a magic piece of paper. With the slump in our purchasing power comes a frustration that can be a blessing if we use it to rethink the role of power in our lives. The discovery that spiritual power is more important than the power of money is a very liberating discovery indeed.

Another ethical challenge is our appetite for social standing, our appetite for prestige over truth, our appetite for success at any cost. Wouldn't it be wonderful if we were able to overcome the high anxiety we sometimes experience over the need to always be politically correct and always have a high social standing?

Perhaps the greatest ethical challenge surrounding poverty and wealth is the temptation that flashes before our eyes every day in myriad ways — *to believe that an extravagant lifestyle brings happiness and the lack of it brings unhappiness.* Nobel Prize-winning economist, Daniel Kahneman of Princeton University, presented a research paper in 2006 showing this belief to be illusory. "Increases in income have mostly a transitory effect on individuals' reported life satisfaction." But we still see it in ads. We see it in movies and television programs. It surrounds us. If every time you see an extravagant lifestyle and then a picture right next to it of happiness and vice versa, you begin to think it is true. You have to fight against that. It is called associative conditioning.

St. Theresa of Avila tells a story in *The Interior Castle* (the 3rd mansion) of a person quite affluent who loses some money on a bad investment. (It was not the subprime mortgage crisis, but it was some loss.) He is simply crushed by it. He is anxious, upset, angry and out of sorts. Theresa asks, how can the Lord possibly get through to that person when he is so wrapped up in himself? What should he do? And she answers, he should admit he has a neurotic attachment to his wealth. He must pray to the Lord to give him freedom in this area.

Today the power and strength of environmental conditioning (riches bring happiness) is far greater than in St. Theresa's day. It influences us in ways we hardly even notice.

Have you ever come in contact with people who think they can buy love? They try to buy it with gifts to their children, with permissions for their kids to do all sorts of unsupervised things. Except for a few brief moments here and there, it is unlikely that they really believe they can buy love that they feel they so desperately need. But they keep trying. Most people who are hungry for love have never tried hard to let the Lord love them and they feel unloved under most circumstances. They are willing to settle for being liked. They can buy attention, even admiration. Yes, love buyers tend to buy everything their children want, but neglect everything their children need. Love buyers get admiration and attention. But admiration and attention are only poor substitutes for real love and they are never quite satisfying. But many love buyers just keep trying.

A middle way of moderation

So we have to work on a right balance or moderation between puritanical suppression and wallowing in materialism.

A proper balance between the two can help us develop a moral compass and religious sensitivity. The gospel of the Lord calls us to seek first the kingdom of heaven. The gospel calls us to look at the lilies of the field which neither sow nor spin, yet our Heavenly Father clothes them in glory. The birds of the air do not engage in commerce, yet our Heavenly Father feeds them.

The presence of wealth is not an automatic sign of divine favor, although there are not a few TV preachers who claim just the opposite. Sensitivity to moral values comes from embracing the gospel and daily following the Lord. The gospels say we are to pray, Speak Lord, your servant is listening. An affluent person prays, Listen Lord, your servant is speaking.

Look at the story of Dives and Lazarus in Luke's Gospel. Dives did not kick old Lazarus. He did not spit on Lazarus. He did not make fun of Lazarus. He did not have Lazarus removed from the doorstep. Dives was condemned for none of these things. Then why was he condemned? Because he barely noticed Lazarus. He simply accepted the world in which Lazarus existed. He just did not really care. He was indifferent. He was too busy with other things.

The opposite of love in the gospels is not hate. It is not caring. Remember in *Gone with the Wind*, Rhett Butler saying to Scarlet, "Frankly, my dear, I don't give a d....") Indifference.

In classical literature, there is the story of King Midas who asked the gods for a special gift. The gift? That whatever he touched would turn to gold. It was called "The Midas Touch." The gods gave him the gift and he walked into the Great Hall for lunch and he picked up an apple and it turned to gold. And he picked up a roll and some roast beef and they both turned to gold. And he realized he could no longer eat anything...but then, much worse, his little daughter whom he loved so much came running in to see him and she ran into his arms and she turned to gold. His desire for gold sucked life right out of her. That's a powerful story.

As a child growing up in the Depression, I remember a family living down the street from us. The father was a banker who lost his bank and livelihood, thus having to move into our somewhat lower middle class neighborhood. They were angry. They were ashamed, aloof and very frustrated. They were never good neighbors. They gave the impression of being a cut above all the rest of us. I left that neighborhood at age 18, never to return and often wondered what happened to that man and his family.

CHAPTER FIVE

The Chief Moral Mandate of Financial Sector Leaders

Part I: The Magnitude of the Economic Crisis

It is important for common folk, you and me, religious and lay leaders to understand how in 2008-2009 the U.S. suddenly ceased to be the economic leader of the world. We are a democratic country. Our government kept saying it would clean up this mess. Many still do not believe them. To make sense of this quagmire, let us try to understand what happened.

In 1991, something unbelievable took place in world politics, namely, the Soviet Union collapsed. What Ronald Reagan called "the evil empire" fell in upon itself. Its collapse was ushered in by the Russian government leaders themselves. (President Reagan, British Prime Minister Margaret Thatcher, and Pope John Paul II surrounded the Soviet power plant and Gorbachev turned the lights out.)

In the year 2008, the United States suddenly ceased to be the economic leader of the world. What caused this great crash of 2008/2009 and the loss of America's leadership, as well as, with the 2010 chief financial crisis (in Portugal, Ireland, Italy, Greece, and Spain – known as PIIGS) in the EU, a geopolitical setback for the West? Basically, American bankers led the way by embracing freedom without restraint, by lack of public virtue, by selfishness and by acting like the rich man Dives in the gospel…just not paying attention, not treating others as they would want to be treated. This may sound harsh, but it is accurate, even if not too many want to hear it. In addition, the American government officials failed to regulate as they should. This is a far greater event than has happened in America for decades and decades.

America loses supremacy in the world

The American financial system is seen to have collapsed. The American government regulatory framework is seen as an enormous failure to curb widespread abuses and corruption. And the bill Congress finally passed in 2010 is considered by many to be too little. Much of the world still looks at us in this fashion. The Obama administration kept the system from a full free fall, but it did collapse and will not fully recover for years. Think of the still-high rate of unemployment.

People argue about what caused this crisis and mostly they say it was housing prices and the subprime mortgage market in the USA. Others say it in a different way, namely, that when you have very, very low interest rates and an awful lot of money available, the temptation is to make more and more loans to less and less credit-worthy clients. In other words, you are inducing people to invest in things you know will fail. That is not ethical. For example, you are a lending agent at a bank and you get paid on the basis of how many loans you make. So at this low interest rate, you can make more money by giving mortgages to people who cannot possibly pay them back. If you are a home buyer, you would not want to be treated like that. Then why did you treat them in this way?

When the mortgage rates started to rise, thousands and thousands of these borrowers could not afford that rise in variable rates with subsequent delinquencies.

Americans, in general, lost one quarter of their net worth in just about a year and a half after June 30, 2007, and no one, even now, sees a return to where we were before. Why? Because the single largest asset of Americans is equity in their homes. Total home equity in the United States at its peak in 2006 was $13 trillion, has dropped to

$8.8 trillion by mid-2008, and continued falling for some time. So many Americans found themselves with negative equity in their homes.

Retirement accounts are the largest household asset of Americans. Roger Altman notes these dropped by at least 22 percent from $10.3 trillion in 2006 to $8 trillion in mid-2008. At the same time, savings and investment assets (apart from retirement savings) lost $1.2 trillion. Pension assets (apart from retirement savings) lost $1.2 trillion. Together these losses totaled a whopping $8.3 trillion. In other words, too many Americans had nothing saved for emergencies, large or small. And many retired people found no option but to return to work (at lesser paying jobs).

By November 2008, the S&P 500 was down 45 percent from its 2007 high.

This crisis reflects the greatest regulatory failure in modern history. Experts still say western capital markets will not return to full health for years. The U.S. financial system is seen by the world as having failed. China is, in some ways, very pleased. This will stop the global shift towards economic deregulation.

The U. S. has remained the most powerful nation on earth for a while longer because its military strength alone ensures this. But America has lost its place as economic leader in the world.

In globalization, not everyone wins

Many observers point out that the longstanding belief that everybody wins in a single world market is no longer widely held. Much of the world blames the U.S. financial excesses for the global recession. So the U.S. model of free market capitalism, with fewer restraints, is out of favor. So much of what you read here is meant to illustrate how enormous our troubles are. The facts narrated here about the economic structure of various nations are taken from experts and are narrated here to help you also understand what we have been up against. If I can learn it, so can you.

Three of the world's largest economies, U.S., the European Union, and Japan have not, it seems, been able to generate a normal cyclical recovery. The global expansion of goods, capital and jobs started reversing. Exports started falling sharply. The World Bank says exports from China, Japan, Mexico, Russia and the U.S. fell by 25 percent or more in the year ending 2008.

Capital flows were plunging. Experts say emerging markets received only $165 billion in net positive capital inflow in the year 2009, down from $461 billion in 2008.

Immigrant workers have been returning home in droves. Japan and Spain have been offering them cash to leave. Malaysia has been forcing them out.

Countries in Africa have been hardest hit. Democratic Congo, as well as the Central African Republic are in political chaos. Central African Republic could not pay its civil servants. It was literally falling apart. The Democratic Congo was hardly able to import essential food and fuel. A World Bank study estimates that 53 million people living in emerging markets fell back into absolute poverty in 2009. Then Russia and Iran were also hurt very, very badly. Iran was losing money on every barrel of oil it sells. Russia has been too dependent on a single giant source of income…oil and gas. Its economy, too, has been in trouble. The debts of Portugal, Ireland, Italy, Greece and Spain (PIIGS) seemed unbearable.

Only China seems to have prevailed. China's growth, we are told, did not at first diminish. It is becoming clear that the U.S./China relationship emerges as the most important bilateral one in the world. The two nations have very similar geopolitical interests. Neither China nor America wants Iran to acquire nuclear weapons. Neither wants Korea to become destabilized. Neither wants Pakistan to become a failed state.

In summary, the free market capitalism, globalization and deregulation which had been rising for thirty years have all now ended.

What does this new world look like?

Free-market capitalism is in enormous decline.

In its place has come **state capitalism**, a system where the state functions as the leading economic actor and uses markets primarily for political gain. For example, it has been said that the economic capital of the United States ceased for a time to be New York City and became Washington, D. C. (the White House). And with that, came the injection of politics into economic decisions. A bad deal!

State capitalism, it is pointed out by Altman, has four primary agencies:

1. **National oil corporations** – the thirteen largest oil companies in the world measured by their reserves are owned and operated by governments, not multinational corporations such as BP, Chevron, ExxonMobil, Shell or Total. These companies include: Saudi Arabia's Saudi Aramco; the National Iranian Oil Company; Petróleos de Venezuela, S.A.; Russia's Gazprom and Rosneft; the China National Petroleum Corporation; Malaysia's Petronas and Brazil's Petrobras. State-owned companies control more than 75 percent of global oil reserves and production.

2. **State-owned enterprises** – Altman wisely notes governments don't just regulate the market. These

state-owned enterprises help bolster political leaders. What are state-owned enterprises? Think of Angola's Endiama (diamonds), Azerbaijan's AzerEnerji (electricity generation), Kazakhstan's Kazatomprom (uranium), and Morocco's Office Chérifien des Phosphates. Then also think of Russia's fixed line telephone and arms-export monopolies. Think of China's aluminum monopoly, power-transmission duopoly, major telecommunications companies and airlines. Think of India's national railroad.

3. In some developing countries, **large companies remain in private hands, but rely on government patronage** in the form of credit, contracts, and subsidies. Here you have corruption, bribery and everything that happens when you drive out competition. For example, in Russia any large business must have favorable relations with the state in order to succeed. National champions are controlled by a small group of oligarchs who are personally in favor with the Kremlin. The companies Norilsk Nickel (mining), Novolipetsk Steel and NMK Hlding (metallurgy), and Evraz, SeverStal and Metallionvest (steel) fall into this category. In China, the same applies.

Variations of the privately owned but government-favored national champions have cropped up elsewhere: Cevital (agroindustries) in Algeria, Vale (mining) in Brazil, Tata (cars, steel and chemicals) in

India, Tnuva (meat and dairy) in Israel, Solidere (construction) in Lebanon, and the San Miguel Corporation (food and beverage) in the Philippines.

4. The task of financing these companies has fallen in part to **Sovereign Wealth Funds** (SWFS). These act as repositories for excess foreign currency earned from the export of commodities or manufactured goods. They are more than just bank accounts. They are state-owned investment funds with mixed portfolios of foreign currencies, government bonds, real estate, precious metals and a stake in lots of companies, foreign and domestic. The Kuwait Investment Authority, now the world's fourth-largest SWF, was founded in 1953. I am told the term "sovereign wealth fund" was first coined in 2005, reflecting a recognition of these funds' growing significance. Since then, several countries have joined the game: Dubai, Libya, Qatar, South Korea and Vietnam.

It is hard to argue with the view that all of this makes markets less competitive and less productive. Only free markets can produce durable prosperity. Please note that since the great collapse of 2008, governments of the world's wealthiest countries have been intervening in their economies and taking ownership of private assets. The U.S. and European governments know that to maintain popular support they must promise to return these large enterprises and banks into private hands once they've been restored to health. *Not so in other places.*

New York City was the world's financial capital. It is now no longer even the financial capital of the United States. Washington is. Experts say a similar shift of economic responsibility is taking place throughout the world: from Shanghai to Beijing, from Dubai to Abu Dhabi, from Sydney to Canberra, from São Paulo to Brasilia, from Mumbai to New Delhi. And in London, Moscow and Paris, where finance and politics coexist there is the same shift occurring toward government.

The result: *Deep state intervention in the economy means a door is opening to bureaucratic ways of inefficiency and corruption. This is more likely to hold back growth.*

Now there is much talk about "decoupling," the process whereby emerging economies develop a domestic base to free them from dependence on consumer demand in the U.S. and Europe. Experts say incidences of decoupling are found in Brazil, China, India and Russia.

PART II – The Question for Financial Sector Leaders: Am I My Brother's Keeper?

Economic theory in the last thirty years has harmed human flourishing.

To make the statement that economic theory in the last thirty years has harmed human flourishing should not be taken in isolation. The economic global crisis has simply exposed something in the underlying culture that has been there for decades and that is: This culture promotes a selfish lifestyle, a decline in religion and a changed system of values. It is more a culture of self-absorption and less a culture of responsibility. In this culture, it was simply easier for so many otherwise decent people to be inattentive to what they were doing...buying and selling super-complicated financial products. Add to this the pace at which financial trans-actions occur and the pressure on managers. It is not hard to understand *the ethical problems surrounding the economic collapse were easy to disregard, set aside or miss completely.*

We will see in Chapter Seven how the development of economic theory (the Chicago School) in the last thirty years has been harmful to the human condition. If we only take away, at this point, the thought of what a malignant disease a free market based on self-interest is, it will be enough.

We were moving toward globalization and it was thought that everyone would gain if we all went down that path. Not so.

The main moral mandate after the economic collapse

Lest the reader think we are oversimplifying, let it be stated here that the ethical problems surrounding the economic collapse are so enormous that no one person can get their hands totally around them at the present time. Theories are in conflict. Issues are extremely complex. Why didn't economists foresee the financial meltdown? After all, they are experts. Yale University's well known economist, Robert Schiller, thinks that the failure to foresee the financial meltdown was due to the economists themselves being afraid to speak up against the majority view.

But despite the complexity at heart, there is one moral mandate for financial institutions that needs attention right now. There are many in the financial world who are not ready or willing and there may be many in the political world who are not ready or willing to embrace it.

That first moral mandate for financial institutions is to embrace Golden Rule morality. That means abandoning the reigning rule of self interest and acknowledging that I am my brother's keeper.

John J. DiJulio Jr. says it succinctly: "Golden Rule morality is a requisite condition for financial stability." He continues, "Transnational free markets must be...viewed as fair markets, in which investing involves risks but is not easily rigged against anyone or any group."

Mario Draghi, chair of the G20's Financial Stability Board and also Bank of Italy Governor, called the self-interest position "an ideological bias." He was addressing the May 2010 meeting of the Pontifical Academy of Social Sciences in Vatican City. At the same meeting, Professor Jose Raga of the University of Madrid (echoing the views of many) said the "crisis (looks) to be moral rather than economic." The moral failure, in his view, was on the doorstep of banks which knew or should have known they should not be acting in the way they did.

Mary Anne Glendon, Harvard professor, at the meeting, pointed to self-interest views that make it harder to see "the moral element of their actions." This urge to allow selfishness to flourish is so strong, a special effort must be made to resist it and to do what is morally right.

The difficulty of doing this is pointed out by Christopher Lowney who for seventeen years was a J.P. Morgan banker and managing director in New York, Singapore, London and Tokyo: "The question is: What is a Catholic to do if he or she is in the executive suite and realizes what's happening when toxic assets are bundled or in a mortgage firm where the unwary and unsuitable are being granted impossible mortgages?"

He concludes, "To someone with executive power and responsibility, the only question is: do they have the courage to leave? Frankly, we saw people who preferred to leave rocks unturned rather than ask difficult questions. When things are going apparently well in terms of earnings and your own bonus, there can be a strong incentive not to have the moral courage to ask these difficult questions."

Finally he notes, "The rather more painful circumstance is that of people further down the line. There, speaking truth to power, can involve a huge amount of personal risk and people aren't sure what the calculus will hold for them. It is the people in those circumstances who are our real moral heroes."

It is important for all of us to reflect on this matter of fear. It is an issue we sometimes call human respect. We need to understand how fear can impede people from speaking out, especially in giant corporations. It is an urgent issue. In particular, economists and others in the financial industry need to learn to overcome this environmental conditioning and to resist this social manipulation. This requires virtue and wisdom. It should be earnestly prayed for. Lowney said: "Do they have the courage to leave?"

Benedict XVI said it in a slightly different way before the economic collapse: "The economy needs ethics in order to function correctly – not any ethics whatsoever, but an ethics which is people-centered." (*Caritas in Veritate*, 45).

Let us listen to Lowney: "Given the seductions of corporate life, it is kind of a rat race and in a normal subconscious level you give yourself over to this idea that I will measure my whole life on a comparative basis: Am I getting ahead of that guy? Is my bonus bigger than that guy? Do I have more power than that guy?" He continues: "I am trying to say these demons work in our lives: greed, desire for power and prestige, winning, wanting to be in control. All of these things can take hold of us in a way to sometimes have us make very dumb decisions."

Most everyone will agree we have too many leaders of nations and giant corporations who aspire to what is good, but do what is expedient. And they believe too much in the primacy of self-interest. This is sort of a "false consciousness." Onlookers can see them lacking in virtue, but that is hard for them to see it this way. The excuse: "I did the best I could." Can you notice the harm caused by their believing unethical decisions are only wrong when they do not succeed? The call for virtue is urgently needed, especially to wake up people whom Lowney describes thusly: "Frankly, we saw people who preferred to leave rocks unturned rather than to ask the difficult questions." They did not think they were their brother's keeper.

So on one hand, you see the CEO and other top executives of Goldman Sachs, testifying in spring 2010 before Congress and looking very greedy and guilty indeed. And on the other hand, as Lowney says: "Many of the most principled people I ever worked with were at J.P. Morgan on Wall Street. And I have no doubt that continues to be case: people who have plenty of opportunities every day to make dreadful – from a moral perspective – choices and instead made very tough decisions."

So it isn't just you and me who need a change of heart. It is financial sector leaders who need a change of mind and heart. Yes, they need to have qualms about abandoning the Golden Rule. They need to feel remorse for the part they played in the economic collapse – by omission or commission. They need to lament what happened. They need to reproach themselves (some, not all) for not being their brother's keeper. They need to abandon the belief which Alan Greenspan espoused in the past, namely that self-interest will promote the common good. They need to bring morality further into the office. Emeritus professor Charles Wilbur at Notre Dame University comments: "even more encouraging is the growing recognition that economies require ethical behavior in addition to self-interest." People are now saying that even Adam Smith was of the persuasion that individual greed cannot be the basis for social good. Pope Benedict said the same thing in a different way: "If each one thinks only of his or her own interest, the world can only go to ruin."

For those who are reading this chapter on the chief moral mandate for business, a question will naturally arise. Should economic and political leaders adopt a more moderate lifestyle? Steve Fishman wrote in *New York Magazine* on November 30, 2008, about Richard Fuld, Jr., CEO of now bankrupt Lehman Brothers:

> "At night, Fuld has trouble sleeping. Most of the time, he lives in Greenwich, Connecticut, in one of his five houses. He can wander through the 20 rooms, eight bedrooms, the pool house, tennis court, squash court. Mostly, he sits and replays Lehman's calamitous end. What could I have done differently, he thinks. In certain conversations what should I have said, what could I have done? He now wonders how did it go so disastrously wrong? "

Should such leaders adopt a more moderate lifestyle? And should they be more mindful of those who have less? Adopting a moderate lifestyle is a conscious decision which the whole family should be involved in making. This gives leaders an opportunity to witness to their sons and daughters that all of us were especially blessed being born and living in a prosperous time, even with an economic downturn. It gives all of us an opportunity to teach our children that what is more important than anything else is being family, caring for one another and caring for those in need. It gives us an opportunity to say, even if someone does not set out to harm anyone, that it is wrong to simply follow one's own self-interest. Benedict said it this way: "Self-fulfillment is a contradiction and is too little for us. We have a loftier destination." That realization, when it dawns on us, is the beginning of virtue.

Montesquieu was a guiding light to the founders of our country. He said the greatest danger to a self-governing society was too much prosperity because it would tempt its citizens to put self-restraint, self-discipline and self-moderation aside and forget about one's neighbor, justice and honesty and integrity and hard work and control over greed. Yes, forget we are our brother's keeper. We forget the Golden Rule.

Perhaps it might be appropriate to conclude with some thoughts from Dietrich Bonhoeffer, the Lutheran pastor martyred by the Nazis in World War II. In 1938, he published a little work called *The Cost of Discipleship*. He talked about cheap grace and expensive grace. "Cheap grace is grace without discipleship, grace without the cross, grace without Jesus Christ, living and incarnate."

Bonhoeffer could see the gospel's rich young man in so many in his own time as material prosperity returned to

Germany with the rise of totalitarianism at the expense of justice. And he might see the rich young man in so many people today when they are oblivious to the needs of their neighbor (at home or across the world) and when their jobs become more important than their character. A person's character is revealed in what we do when no one is watching. Yes, we can remain in a cheap grace relationship to God, but it will only harm us and harm the common good. In other words, we should use our jobs and the good life as God wants us to, namely, not as owning the material goods ourselves to do with as we like, but given to us in stewardship only for a short time. "Come Lord Jesus" into our lives, into our national economy and into our world.

Postscript: Much of the economic data in this chapter is extracted from three marvelous articles in the July/ August 2009 issue of *Foreign Affairs*. They are: "The Great Crash, 2008" by Roger Altman, formerly U.S. Deputy Treasury Secretary in 1993-1994; "State Capitalism Comes of Age" by Ian Bremmer, President of Eurasia Group; and "Globalization in Retreat" also by Roger Altman. The moral reflections come from both me and a variety of other sources, including the authors mentioned in Chapter Six. See also Montesque, John diJulio, John Hughey's *The Holy Use of Money* (Garden City: Doubleday, 1986, and many others.

How All the Trouble Started

There are lots of books and articles explaining the financial collapse, first in the banking system and then the failure of so many other firms resulting in loss of jobs, savings and even the sudden loss of hope for the future. For you and me who read this, the crisis hit home in the terrible financial damage done to your household and mine and to small and big businesses resulting from the housing collapse and the credit market collapse. Many authors point out that it was America's bankers and businessmen, on one hand, and our government failing to properly regulate these credit markets on the other which has put the American model of free market capitalism under a cloud.

How did all this trouble get started?

The financial system collapsed. The government regulators failed to curb widespread abuses, both in derivatives and subprime mortgages. *America has lost its economic primacy in the world, just as you and I have lost much in terms of jobs, savings and hope. This economic crisis is global and it will go on longer than most of us think.* America has to now focus inward because of unemployment and all our other troubles. Much of the world blames the financial excesses of our American bankers for the world crisis, and rightly so, as well as our government's failure to regulate and rightly so. The good will toward President Obama mitigated some of this at first, but not by very much.

What we are trying to do here is to help you understand how we got into this mess because it will help you personally climb out of this hole by righting your spiritual priorities and freeing you from anxieties, giving you the strength to move forward in a hopeful way. The economic collapse is a test to determine whether we are serving God or mammon.

So we begin with the question: How did all this trouble get started? Lots of people have written much, but perhaps the most helpful insights are found in several sources. The first is Gillian Tett's book entitled *Fool's Gold* which puts the spotlight on derivatives. She is an award-winning financial journalist with a degree in anthropology. The second is Roger Lowenstein's best seller entitled *The End of Wall Street* which is most helpful in understanding the huge unethical debacle of sub-prime mortgages. The third is Michael Lewis' *The Big Short: Inside the Doomsday Machine* telling the story of what happened when lenders got to Wall Street to package all of this. Then there is also Andreas Kinneging's *The Geography of Good and Evil*, awarded the Socrates prize as the best Dutch philosophical work in 2006. He teaches law at the University of Leiden in Holland. The insights of all these authors are very important and many other authors point to the very same things.

It all started, says Tett, with bankers at J.P. Morgan who were looking for new "products" to peddle to make more money in the early 1980s and how they came up with exotic financial products known as credit derivatives. We will see how derivatives involved currency trading at the start and then grew to just about every aspect of the business known across the globe. We will describe some of it here. It is important we understand that the great banks and financial institutions of the world were involved: Chase, Citigroup, Bank of America, UBS, Deutsche Bank, Barclay's Bank of London, Merrill Lynch, Lehman Brothers and insurance giants such as AIG and Fannie Mae and Freddie Mac and many others.

Tett points out that this economic collapse was not triggered by a recession or war or other traditional events.

That is the way it usually happens. This collapse, however, was self-inflicted by the *banking community*, starting in America, and the *failure of our government oversight bodies* to regulate those bankers. The blame cannot be put on just a few bad, greedy individuals, although there were some of those. The blame, says Tett, must be put on the investment system itself, as well as the watchdog regulatory structures of government and the lack of oversight. Many mortgage lenders and bankers *abandoned the public and private virtues of prudence, moderation, balance and any concern for the common good*, says Tett. This was a huge ethical failing. Instead, they relied on complex mathematical models which were based on what they now themselves say were "a ridiculously limited set of data" and which they embraced as an infallible guide. Many of them believed selfishness as a virtue as long as you do not mean to harm others. Kinneging who wrote before the financial collapse said straightforwardly that if business people do not believe everyone (including themselves) has inclinations to evil, that must be protected against, chaos...will ensue. He was right.

A fundamental principle of anthropology

Because these new products were so arcane and hard to understand, the financial gurus did what, in anthropology, is called exercising the function of elites. Tett says: "Elites try to maintain their power, not simply by garnering wealth, but also by dominating the mainstream ideologies, in terms of both what is said and what is not discussed." Bankers sat in their silos. They said: We'll make lots of money. Everything is okay. Everybody will prosper. Don't think anything is bad. And those elites dominated everyone below and above them so they did not ask questions. Regulators sat in their silos placing blind faith in the creed of risk dispersion. There is no need for more outside regulation, they said, and need for only self-regulation. Any one who disagreed with them was laughed to scorn. Congress was self-interested. The whole financial community was in its own great big silo separated from the rest of society. Many smaller investment firms and trust funds cannot be blamed for believing the "big fish" would not lead them this far astray. This was capitalism gone mad. It was hysteria.

Kinneging puts it this way: "The most important element of man's humanity is moral conscience. It is that which makes him truly human, allows him to become civilized and to be free." Our inclination to greed and excessive self-seeking are always present. "For this reason, society will never be able to cope without social control mechanisms and a body of legal instruments to keep man on the right path." This was lacking.

The basics at the beginning

In the early 1980s, J. P. Morgan, along with several other famous banks, jumped into these newfangled derivatives which then exploded. Some ten years later, by 1994, the total national value of derivatives contracts on J. P. Morgan's books was estimated to be $1.7 trillion. These activities were generating half of the bank's trading revenue. If you make .02 percent on each contract it is a small amount, but it adds up to huge sums with great volume.

It is important, says Tett, to note most members of the banking and investment world themselves had absolutely no clear idea how these strange new derivatives were producing phenomenal sums, let alone what so called swaps groups actually did. You would think their consciences would have made them suspicious, but not so. It was a good way to make money. Where were their boards of directors? Those who worked in the area liked to revel in its aura of mystery. *These bankers referred to their experiments as "innovation," meaning the invention of new ways of generating returns.* Peter Hancock, the leader of the group at J.P. Morgan, often said to his subordinates, "You will have to make at least half your revenues each year from a product which did not exist before."

A derivative is, on the most basic level, a bet on the future value of an asset. It is a contract whose value derives from some other asset such as a bond, a stock or quantity of gold. Those who buy and sell derivatives are each making a bet on the future value of that asset. The bet can be a way to protect yourself against undesirable price swings, for example, farmers selling futures, on contracts in grain. There is nothing intrinsically wrong with derivatives if used prudently and regulated wisely with sufficient collateral or assets to cover risks. And the idea has been around for a long time.

Here's an example Tett uses. Let's say that on a particular day the pound to dollar exchange rate is such that one British pound buys $1.50. So Joe is going to make a trip from England to the United States in six months and he wants to be sure that he can buy dollars at that rate just before the trip. So he might enter into an agreement to exchange one thousand pounds at a bank in six months time at $1.50 per pound, no matter what the actual exchange rate is then. And he agrees the trade must happen no matter what the rate of exchange at the time. That is a *future*. There is nothing wrong with futures if used prudently and regulated wisely.

Or he may agree to pay a fee (let's say $25) to have the *option* to make the exchange at the $1.50 rate which he would decide not to exercise if the rate actually became more favorable.

Tett points out that although the very complex derivatives of the 1990s were new, there were simpler versions of derivatives trading going all the way back to clay tablets from Mesopotamia in 1750 B.C., with futures and options trading. In the 12th and 13th Centuries, English monasteries that raised sheep entered into futures contracts with foreign merchants to sell wool up to twenty years in advance. In the 17th Century, Holland's tulip prices began to rise substantially. The merchants frantically bought and sold tulip futures leading to a bubble that ended in a spectacular crash.

In 1849, the Chicago Board of Trade began to allow buying and selling of futures and options on wheat and corn, cattle and hogs, etc. Farmers often lock in a specific price for grain "for September delivery."

What ushered in a bold new era of derivatives innovation was the idea to expand derivatives beyond commodities, (corn, beans, wool, livestock) to currency trading, to homes, etc. The value of foreign currencies, (which had been pegged to the dollar) after World War II, became free floating. That led to unpredictable swings in exchange rates. Inflation in the U.S. peaked at 13.2 percent in 1981 and it made investors try to find ways to protect themselves from high interest rates.

The prime rate in the U.S. rose to 20 percent in June 1981. So now you could buy derivatives which offered you the right to purchase currencies at specific exchange rates in the future.

Peter Hancock's group in the 1980s at J. P. Morgan specialized in another creative version of derivatives known as "swaps." Let's take a simple example of two home owners, owner A and owner B. They both have a $500,000 ten-year mortgage. Owner A has a fixed rate of 8 percent and owner B has a floating rate. If owner A thinks that rates are going to go down and doesn't want to pay the fixed 8 percent, and owner B thinks they are going to go up so he would like to have a fixed rate of 8 percent, they could swap their payments for as long as they agreed to. *As Warren Buffett likes to say, this is gambling, pure and simple.*

Note, too, that after the financial crash of 1929, bringing the Great Depression to America and the rest of the world, there was a popular backlash against Wall Street. The Glass Steagall Act was passed by Congress and signed into law, forcing banks to split off their commercial banking business from the capital markets operation (trading of debt and equity securities...derivatives). This was stern government regulation!

The crucial point about derivatives is that they can, on one hand, help investors reduce risk or they can create a great deal more risk. Everything depends on how they are used, how to determine risk, and the motives and skills of those who trade in them. So J.P. Morgan's New York headquarters in the 1980s could not (because of Glass Steagall regulations) play capital markets, but

its London office could because England was not subject to Glass Steagall and had a more hands-off attitude
toward regulation. The London traders had greater
power and freedom and they could make a lot of
money fast, take far greater risks or... Tett says few of
the higher ups at Morgan knew, in detail, how the
swaps teams worked.

Gambling with a Triple-A rating

Morgan was one of the very few banks with a top AAA
rating and that assured clients that the bank could
stand by its trades. By the early 1990s, the swaps
department accounted for almost half the bank's trading revenues.

Tett points out the head of the swaps groups once
explained to a reporter from *Fortune* that his group was
like "the spaceship Galileo heading for Planet Jupiter...
*It would be something in which you would get beyond
binary risk and into a combination of risks such as
interest rates and currencies.*" Hancock gave an example of an oil company which was afraid of oil prices
dropping and interest rates rising. To hedge, it would
buy an oil price floor and an interest rate cap...but
maybe the company would like something a little
cheaper. "In that case, we could do a contract that
would pay out only if oil prices are low and interest
rates are high at the same time."

By the early 1990s, U.S. government bank regulators knew that many of their rules had been drafted *before* the explosion of derivatives innovation. They, for example, determined levels of reserves banks must have if they were engaging in derivatives activities. *But the problem was the regulators couldn't get good estimates of the risks* involved and so many kept saying everything is fine. *So their rules for levels of bank reserves were way too low.* The elites maintained their power by making sure their views prevailed and naysayers were marginalized.

Now there was an industry body to represent the swaps world and it was called the International Swaps and Derivatives Association. And the first thing the ISDA did was conduct a survey of the market. In 1987, ISDA guessed the total volume of derivative contracts was $865 billion. That shocked western government officials. So in 1987, the U.S. Commodities Futures Trading Commission wanted to regulate interest rates and currency swaps in the same way that it monitored commodities derivatives. The ISDA lobbied Congress against this and won. So government regulation did not happen as it should have. A sad day.

It was a crazy period because the ISDA now said that the rules should be *written by industry itself* and upheld by voluntary mutual accord. Alan Greenspan, the Chairman of the Federal Reserve, liked voluntariness

91

because he strangely believed that if everyone followed their own self-interest everything would go fine. As mentioned above, he was a disciple of Ayn Rand whose books in the 1950s recommended what she called the "virtue of selfishness." He believed if everybody is selfish, everything will work out well. I know that sounds dumb, but Alan Greenspan believed it and so did lots of others because it fit their purposes...make a lot of money and don't worry about anyone else. You do not have to care about them, only yourself. That belief blinds one to virtue and vice. Kinneging points out that only the foolish believe our hearts are not inclined to evil.

Remember a basic rule of anthropology: elites gain and maintain power not only by money, but also by making sure their view (Greenspan and Bernanke) dominated and prevailed. So if you were at a lower level in the industry, you were told to keep your views to yourself or you would be in trouble.

By now all the great banks and stock market firms not only of America, but the world were caught up in the derivatives movement: Chase Manhattan, Citigroup, UBS, Deutsche Bank, Wells Fargo, Bank of America, Bear Stearns, etc.

Now let's focus on the gigantic mortgage market. The assumption of the elite was that home prices would continue to rise as they had, more or less, ever since

World War II. We talked earlier about the *democratization of credit*. Now let's look at it more carefully through the eyes of Roger Lowenstein, *The End of Wall Street*. Especially interesting is his portrayal of Angelo Mozilo, CEO of Countrywide Financial, who believed every citizen was worthy of a mortgage, a noble-sounding idea. In 2003 at a Harvard University symposium, he eloquently spoke of "expanding the American dream of home ownership." He insisted on mortgages with no money down. How? By writing first mortgages for 80 percent of home value and "piggy backing" a loan for the rest.

By 2005, Countrywide's shares rose fourfold and "over the ensuing years, Mozilo personally reaped $447 million in stock sales." Borrowers even had the option of reducing at will the amount of first year monthly payments. But these "teaser loans" came with a catch. If you got a $150,000 mortgage, your payments could be $125 a month for a year, but after that the payment would jump to $876 per month.

Up front, loan officers would "assist" applicants (coach them to lie) and the loans would be approved. Sometimes no documentation was required. The option ARM was widespread. Lowenstein says: "Many of the borrowers failed to grasp that the option ARM was a trap in which they could end up owing more than they had borrowed." Soon Washington Mutual joined the game.

Mozilo started with marvelous rhetoric (let us remedy income inequality) but he had to know this was a scam. And the people to get hurt were the very poor Mozilo claimed he was helping. He closed his eyes to the ordinary rules of finance in response to a financial problem and made millions in the process. An indication of his freewheeling ways were the buckets of "sweetheart mortgages" he handed out to influential people, for example, two former Secretaries of HUD and two former CEOs of Fannie Mae.

If Lowenstein tells the story of unethical subprime mortgages, Michael Lewis (*The Big Short – Inside the Doomsday Machine*) narrates what happened when the lenders got Wall Street to package them. A common form was CDOs (collateralized debt obligations) which, in this case, were "just a pile of triple B-rated mortgage bonds." The bonds were backed by subprime mortgages. And Wall Street convinced the rating agencies (Moody's and Standard and Poor) to upgrade them to triple-A or double-A or A. Michael Lewis says of these CDOs, "That's a fraud. Maybe you can't prove it in a court of law, but it is a fraud."

And they changed the bond market terminology to disguise what was going on. The word "tranches" was used instead of "floors" and the risky ground floor was called the "mezzanine." And this riskiest (mezzanine) layer of subprime mortgages was called a "structured finance CDO." Yes, that is fraud! These people were engaged "in just blatant fraud." The lower and middle income people were the least protected and the most likely to get ripped off. "Targeting unsophisticated residents of borderline neighborhoods smacked of exploitation. One mortgage shop in Baltimore worked 4:00 p.m. to midnight, the better to catch customers at home." In other words, the mortgage lenders knew these were loans they should not give. That is morally wrong because the poor get hurt even worse. Neither the families nor the lenders worried about the risk because it was blindly assumed they would simply refinance the loan at the end of the teaser rate.

And there was another factor illustrated in Barbara Ehrenreich's *Bright-Sided: How the Relentless Promotion of Positive Thinking Has Undermined America*. She is talking about the huge popularity of positive thinking. Think of secular motivational speakers whose predecessors were Mary Baker Eddy, William James, and Norman Vincent Peale. They have taught people to embrace "the law of attraction," namely, you only have to think something or want something bad enough to get it. If you are Mozilo, you will steadfastly refuse to consider bad things might happen like mortgage defaults. Only positive thinking is allowed. And many believed the prosperity preachers (Joel Osteen, T. D. Jakes, Creflo Dollar and Rhonda Byrne) because "God caused the bank to ignore my credit score and bless me with my first house." And if you are a poor minority and you have been denied credit for a long time, this easy mortgage market must have seemed to you like the good Lord's intervention in your life. You just have to believe. But it was self-delusion and as Ehrenreich says: "Someone was offering tricky mortgages to people of dubious means, someone was bundling up these mortgage debts and selling them as securities to investors throughout the world, someone who was expecting to make sizable profits by doing so." The motivational speaker, Tony Robbins, in 2008, told Larry King that he was coaching securities traders who were "the smartest minds around."

Negative opinions were chased out and chastised. Only positive bright thoughts were allowed. For example, CEO Richard Fuld of Lehman Brothers fired the head of his real estate division who warned him that "the bubble" was about to burst. Lehman Brothers went bankrupt some twenty months later. A government official, Armando Falcon, issued a warning in 2003 that Fannie Mae and Freddie Mac were in very bad shape and there could be a financial meltdown. The White House tried to get him fired.

And they all assumed that the incredible rise in home prices since the 1950s would continue, when, lo and behold, in 2006 in Las Vegas and Miami and San Francisco and then Southern California, home prices stalled. This began to trigger a wave of subprime defaults (people could not make their mortgage payments) and some began abandoning their mortgages when their house was worth less than what they owed on the mortgage. Some banks then, interestingly enough, turned to the derivatives market to reduce their risk. They purchased credit default swaps which promised to redeem any default losses on the mortgage bonds. They did not know what enormous risks they were taking.

Tett points out that in January 2006, folks launched an index for tracking these offerings and their values. It was sort of like the Dow Jones and was called ABX. *"Why didn't someone (either regulators or people in the business) blow the whistle?" And the answer, says Tett, comes from anthropology. The elites gain and maintain power not only by money, but by making sure that their view dominated and prevailed. Their view was: this will all work very well. So be quiet!* Kinneging would say they forgot about original sin, our proclivity to close our eyes and pretend we just do not see.

In early 2006, small groups began spotting something odd: some of the data in the mortgage database suggested the pace of defaults on risky mortgages was starting to rise. This seemed strange and did not fit what they thought were the normal economic rules. At the same time, banks and other lenders were passing out lots and lots of shaky mortgages which were becoming riskier and riskier. These loans were repackaged into more and more CDOs (collateralized debt obligations) in order to make up for declining profit margins.

And these were bundled and the products were sold creating huge masses of super senior risk – and guess what. They bought insurance against the super-senior risk from places like AIG. Remember that in 2004, the U.S. Securities and Exchange Commission's five members voted unanimously to lift the leverage ratio control, namely, the controls on the amount of assets a brokerage house could hold on its balance sheet relative to its core equity. The UBS bankers in Europe developed mathematical models that said super-senior would never lose more than 2 percent of its value, even in the worst cases. Nonsense! This defied all prudence and common sense.

In 2006, home prices across America started to slide. In October, the famous home builder, Kara Homes, filed for bankruptcy.

How does this work? Let us take a simple example. You borrow too much on a new house, but at first it is okay because you can make your "teaser rate" monthly payment at its current low rate of interest. However, home prices drop and you cannot refinance. So you now cannot make the much larger payments. So the bank takes the house back and you have to move out. The bank cannot sell the house for the amount of the loan, so it, too, loses money. And the bank needs money to pay its bills, but no other bank will loan it money. This happens on so many mortgages the bank declares bankruptcy. Other banks do the same. People want to take their money out of the bank and the bank has no cash. The elites tried to say everything is okay, but now nobody believes them.

In June 2007, a crisis hit a hedge fund connected to Bear Stearns. J. P. Morgan now threatened to call in its loans. Disaster was near. In mid-July, another tsunami appeared as Deutsche Industrie Bank (IKB), a medium-size lender in Dusseldorf, Germany, started to go under. Would anybody help supply new sources of funds? Nobody did until the German government stepped in. As with the Bear Stearns bailout, this was only a temporary reprieve.

On August 6, 2007, American Home Mortgage Investment Corporation filed for bankruptcy. Now the commercial paper market was starting to get jittery.

Tett says it was then that the Bank of England, the Bank of Japan, the Central Bank of Canada and the Swiss National Bank started to also get jittery. *The Federal Reserve kept making statements that the problems were "contained." Remember what elites do. They control what people believe.* Investors were dumping anything that might contain default risk. They were heading for the safest assets around. Countrywide, America's largest independent mortgage lender, on August 15, 2007, said its rate of foreclosure on subprime loans was roaring upward. Now real trouble came as many banks stopped lending money to any other banks or institutions that looked at all risky.

The government intervenes

On August 31, 2007, then President George Bush stood in the Rose Garden with Treasury Secretary Henry Paulson. Adjustable mortgage rates were climbing and defaults were rising enormously. Democratization of credit had failed so many! The then President Bush tried to calm the nation saying: "This market has seen tremendous innovation in recent years, as new lending products made credit available to more people. For the most part, this has been a positive development...this has led some homeowners to take out loans larger than they could afford based on overly optimistic assumptions about the future performance of the housing market. Others may have been confused by the terms of their loan or misled by irresponsible lenders." The President only offered some simple band-aid solutions.

Then in September, in England, the fifth largest British lender called Northern Rock announced it had gone to the Bank of England to seek emergency support. On October 11, just as Citicorp and J. P. Morgan were trying to create a Superfund, the famous Moody's cut its ratings on $32 billion worth of mortgage-backed bonds which were issued in 2006 and had carried a medium-risk rating. They said they might downgrade $20 billion more of mortgage-backed bonds that carried a AAA stamp.

The entire credit structure was built on the guess that AAA was ultra-safe and AA almost rock solid. Now this was all crumbling.

At the beginning of 2008, UBS, Merrill Lynch and Citibank all reported huge write-downs on credit assets, totaling about $53 billion just for those three banks.

Then Bear Stearns found itself in horrible shape and J. P. Morgan Chase cut a deal to buy Bear Stearns for $2 a share with the Federal Reserve taking $30 billion of Bear Stearns' assets. Remember that in October of 2007, Bear Stearns stock had been trading around $130 a share. Timothy Geithner, New York Federal Reserve Chairman, pulled this deal off at $2 a share! He was later named Secretary of Treasury in the Obama administration! Yes, Geithner was part of that elite!

In February 2008, *AIG finally admitted it did not have the reserves it would need to meet claims.* It announced $43 billion of write-downs of super-senior assets, even more than at Citicorp and UBS. *Lehman Brothers then collapsed on Sunday, September 11, 2008 and at the prospect of AIG collapsing, the money market panicked.* Tett notes calmly, "The three events produced the perfect market storm." The markets went into a freefall.

The next logical step, if this crash continued, was there would be no money coming out of ATM machines. All commerce would be brought to a stand-still. I'll bet those of you who are reading this did not know it was this bad. On the 16th, the Federal Reserve said it would give an $85 billion loan to AIG in exchange for an almost 80 percent share of its com-pany. Note the Federal Reserve had just refused that aid to Lehman Brothers which was now gone. On Monday, the 15th, just before the AIG deal, Bank of America was pushed, by the feds, to buy Merrill Lynch. On October 13, 2008, Treasury Secretary Paulson called nine American bank heads into the U.S. Treasury and they were each given a piece of paper. The feds demanded they sell shares of their banks to the government and they were forcefully told to sign. Secretary of Treasury Paulson said: Take it or leave it. Either you accept voluntary infusion of federal funds or you are out on a limb by yourself. They accepted the funds and the rest is history.

Commercial paper was drying up. Credit was drying up. ATMs would have dried up had the federal government not stepped in.

Summary and conclusions

Tett, Lowenstein, Lewis and many others have wondered how these very bright people trading in derivatives, making subprime mortgages and taking huge risks with other people's money – *how their conscience did not bother them, for what they did was ruin million of Americans' dreams and deflate America's greatness in the eyes of the world*. To say it clearly and simply: It was a egregious violation of the Golden Rule. In so many words they were saying, I am not my brother's keeper. Remember, these young people were trained in some of our finest universities. They were told not to worry, to trust their leaders. Nobody believed in original sin which suggests leaders are especially prone to evil. They possess bright intellects and can understand complex business transactions. They have mastery of high-level mathematical formulas.

A big part of the answer as to why their consciences didn't bother them enough to make a difference lies in that basic principle of anthropology we have repeated about elites. It is tough to go against the tide. It is tough emotionally and financially. It is tough socially because of what behaviorists call environmental conditioning, and that is easy to understand. Most of us live in an environmental bubble and what is inside the bubble conditions us to think the way we think, believe and act unless we have strength enough to make the choice to be deliberately countercultural. For example, if you are a teenager and live in the bubble of MySpace, Facebook, rock stars, Twitter, rappers, drugs, sex and alcohol, you are usually going to believe that this is "the normal way of life." Teenagers will feel they have to live that way. The elites in the media and elsewhere in this teenage world maintain that supremacy.

To not believe what the elite says means you need to be slightly countercultural. A person with strong religious convictions and a solid relationship to God and His people could overcome that environment, but others cannot.

If you live in a silo of bright brokers or lenders or banking people and your purpose is to make as much money as possible and the elites around you and above you make sure their view dominates and prevails ("There is nothing to worry about. Everything is okay."), then, says Tett, you will not realize, except vaguely and occasionally, that what all of you are doing is a violation of prudence, moderation, responsibility, balance and common sense. A violation of virtue!

But the environment tells you over and over again to stop thinking about that. What you will not realize clearly is that you are becoming very insensitive, greedy and selfish and are going to harm others. It is immoral to induce others to purchase mortgages you know they cannot repay. *What is needed to overcome this silo effect is access to a Power greater than the power of the elites.* Many traders and bankers had their private doubts, but too many were swayed by environmental conditioning, by the spirit of their organization. Or they said it was simply too complex to understand and they felt they could not be reasonably expected to figure it out!

If you questioned the rightness of the thinking of the elite where you work, in Countrywide Financial, in Washington Mutual, in your bank or government agency, you would probably be fired or at least not promoted. All of this should provide business schools with the realization that there has to be an enormous effort made in ethical training, in neutralizing environmental conditioning and understanding anthropology required of students if this is not to happen again. *Without virtue all ventures collapse.* To quote again Christopher Lowney, "The only question is: do they have the courage to leave? Frankly, we saw people who preferred to leave rocks unturned rather than ask difficult questions. When things are going apparently well in terms of earnings and your own bonus, there can be a strong incentive not to have the moral courage to ask these difficult questions."

Many of the banking, business and government elites believed in what Ayn Rand called "the virtue of selfishness." They believed that if everyone acts on self-interest everything will work out well. Alan Greenspan believed it and so many others did because it fit their purposes…that ethical theory has to be abandoned (namely, that all persons should seek their own self-interest and all would go well). *It has to be abandoned immediately. It is wrong and destructive of human flourishing.* It is based on the denial of human frailty, a denial of original sin. This means there is a dark side to all of us and greedy selfishness is an ever-present temptation, even in our time in an age of affluence. It needs to be resisted.

What about the elites in this drama? As we saw above, some often describe themselves as feeling invincible, charting new territory, applying new financial services without a touch of humility. They were suffering from what the Greeks called *hubris* or pride/arrogance. There is an old adage: Pride always comes before the fall. That certainly is true here.

What is hubris? It is pride, the conviction that you personally can do almost no wrong and (if you do wrong) that nobody will challenge you. Remember the story of Darius, the great Persian King in the 5th Century B.C. When Athens decided to stand up and declare its independence from Persia, Darius made up his mind to punish them, gathering a great Naval Armada and crossing over to Peloponnesia only to suffer extensive damage to his fleet as a result of a terrible storm. Darius is said to have taken out a huge whip and, whipping the sea, said to the god of the sea, Poseidon: "You will not interfere with my will." Because of his pride, in 490 B.C., his army suffered a huge disaster at the battle of Marathon at the hands of the Athenians who chose freedom over tyranny. The Greeks said Darius lost because of hubris (pride/ arrogance). *The reason the financial world went wacko is also because of hubris on the part of these people who thought they were invincible.* This is Tett's view also and not far from the truth.

That hubris, once again, develops through environmental conditioning. You can be blinded into taking terrible risks with no thought of harm to others if you are reinforced to believe that you are the vanguard of the future. Or if you are at a lower organizational level, you are filled with fear if you don't go along with the elites. In the 21st Century, environments are created with such power they can blind you to moral imperatives at stake. The propaganda machine of Joseph Goebbels was so powerful in Nazi Germany that even good Christian people were blinded into accepting and cooperating with the Holocaust. The Nazis suffered from great hubris.

If, from the 1980s onward, you belonged to the upper tier of the banking fraternity, which is close knit and which feels itself superior and invincible and has success after success, pretty soon it is blinding to those who are part of it. You may otherwise be good people, but here are surrounded by leaders and coworkers who feel themselves untouchable, a new breed, and clearly making huge sums of money. This is heady stuff and you would have to be greatly countercultural to be morally sensitive and courageous enough to stand up to this pressure. This is exceedingly complicated. A good place to reduce the complexity and the opaqueness is to start a strong prayer life (Lord, give me light) and virtue (the ability to see what is the right way to go and follow it).

The great banks and Wall Street have not embraced the Golden Rule even now and there is little evidence to think they intend to...unless they are called to it by prophetic religious voices.

CHAPTER SEVEN

Do Most People Solely Pursue Their Self-Interest?

A Lesson in Behavioral Economics

In the 1930s, America suffered from what was called the Great Depression and, in our time, we are suffering from what is commonly called the Great Recession. For the better part of the last thirty years, the School of Economics at the University of Chicago led by Milton Friedman, Alan Greenspan and others has dominated the world of banking and commerce. It has greatly influenced the world of government regulators, including Congress, the federal bureaucracy and even the White House.

The Chicago School in decline

Regarding this domination, it should come as a surprise to no one that in the aftermath of our recent financial collapse, the self-interest assumption of the Chicago School is being abandoned right and left. As noted earlier, Alan Greenspan saw the economy in shambles and October 23, 2008 said:

> "Those of us who have looked to the self interest of leading institutions to protect shareholder equity, myself included, are in a state of shocked disbelief."

Commissioner J. Thomas Rosch of the U.S. Federal Trade Commission said it this way: "The orthodox and unvarnished Chicago School of Economic Theory is on life support, if not dead."

There is a good summary of this matter by Maurice Stucke, Professor at the University of Tennessee College of Law in the *Santa Clara Law Review* (Vol. 50, 2010).

The defects of the Chicago School thinking have been highlighted for some time by a group of behavioral economists led by the Nobel Prize winner, Daniel Kahneman. They have shown, through experiments, that people just really do not behave like the Chicago School claimed they would, of maximizing profit through self-interest. Various behavioral economists have done many experiments to show that many people forgo self-interest and even sacrifice wealth, preferring fair treatment of others. If the other players are perceived as sharing that influences the outcome of the game.

The Chicago School predicts that financial incentives should motivate behavior. Behavioral experiments, however, clearly indicate humans are not solely motivated by money, but may act contrary to their own self-interest in situations of empathy or social sanctions.

One example is the ultimatum game which is now a common behavioral experiment. In the experiment, you are given $100 and you have to give some portion of that to another person who can either accept it or reject it. If the other person rejects it, neither of you keeps any money at all. If the other person accepts what you offer, both of you keep your portion. This game, as Professor Stucke notes, has been tested in more than twenty countries and found that many, many people offer $50 or half the amount. According to the Chicago School, this is not in their "self-interest." So goodwill or fairness clearly plays a part in their offer of $50 and often trumps self-interest.

Other experiments have been done to show what happens when social norms of fairness and kindness clash with self-interest market norms. In one experiment, there were three groups and all were asked to perform the same task. The first group was not offered any money and was asked to undertake a small task as a favor. In the second group, each member received $5 for doing the task. And in the third group, they received 50 cents for the task. The first group outperformed the market norm groups.

Some experiments show that appealing to conscience and ethical norms deters unwanted behavior more than the threat of penalties. One experiment was of folks preparing their income tax returns. The "conscience" group was provided moral reasons for not cheating (fairness, each of us sharing in the nation's well being, etc.). This had a stronger effect on income reported than in the group that was told there are severe penalties for failure to report income. It seems to indicate that although the threat of punishment, especially among the wealthiest people, can increase tax compliance, appeals to conscience among college-educated taxpayers is more effective. In addition, there are all kinds of further experiments to show that most people simply do not seek self-interest the way the Chicago School says.

But there arises another question then: Should self-interest be "the desired norm? The answer is clearly no. Professor Stucke notes: "Once a country's gross domestic product per capita exceeds a moderate level of income, societies do not become happier as they grow richer."

Gregg Easterbrook in *The Progress Paradox* notes that those who went before us a hundred years ago were not prosperous, but seemed very, very happy while we are prosperous and do not seem very happy. The paradox is why life does not feel better when people have more. Think of what we said earlier about evangelical poverty. It is often pointed out by great saints like Mother Teresa that if we spend time and money on others this is a predictor of greater happiness than simply being selfish.

Behavioral experiments now reinforce this idea. One experiment reported in the March 21, 2008 issue of *Science* magazine showed this. One group was given money in the morning and told to spend it on themselves by the afternoon. And the second group was given the same amount of money and told to give it to someone else or a charity. Guess which group was happier in the afternoon? The one who gave it away.

Professor Stucke logically asks the question: "If we are happier when we give rather than just keep for ourselves, why aren't we more giving and buying less for ourselves?" And the answer is clear. Most affluent folks have the "superstitious belief" that we will be much happier if we keep spending on ourselves and would not necessarily be so happy if we gave money to others. So we keep spending on ourselves, but it does not seem to make us any happier. That is why it is called a "superstitious belief."

It was the ancient philosopher Aristotle who reminded us of why this is so. According to Aristotle, there is a natural check on our desire for food. We keep eating and eating and eating until we can't eat any more and we're full. If we eat any more, we will throw up. He also said that there is a natural check on drinking. We can only drink so much before we pass out. But he reminded us there is no natural limit to the amount of money and goods that we have. At $100,000, we do not throw up or are rendered unconscious. And then there is what we have often referred to as "keeping up with the Jones'." And even though we may sometimes have the feeling inside that we are on a treadmill, we keep the wheels spinning, especially out of envy and partially out of habit. It is environmental conditioning such as we hear repeatedly with the mantra: I want it all. I want it now. And it will not bring us happiness.

If the Great Recession can do anything positive at all, hopefully, it can make you and me and all of us realize that greed, envy, self-interest and lack of self-restraint on spending have not brought us happiness and never will. And now we have the "behavioral economists" joining this chorus. Maybe these economists can convince more Americans than we preachers.

Fundamental sources of happiness

Richard Layard writes in *Happiness: Lessons from a New Science* that behavioral experiments reinforce the notion that there are certain very fundamental sources of human happiness. And greed, envy and self-interest are not among these sources. *The first source is family.* If family goes well, happiness follows. So if our family relationships are not going well, we need to work on them. *The second source of happiness is work or employment.* Many of us realize that doing a good job at work does bring satisfaction and happiness. We also realize that if our place of work has become a pain and drudgery, it is going to be hard to find happiness there. *Having true friends also brings happiness.* We often lament the fact that we have too little time to work on our friendships in the fast paced, impersonal society in which we live. *Good mental health and physical health* also are fundamental sources of happiness. *And personal faith and moral values* help us enormously when we are ill, especially during the end times of our lives. St. Francis was not the first or the last to point out that the *beauty of nature itself* can be a great source of happiness if we nurture it. *Service to the community*, we all know, brings happiness. And that is why it is good to see that the new science of behavioral economics reinforces what we believed when we were younger and wiser, but maybe have forgotten in the economic foolishness that we have lived in the past several decades. Selfishness is not

115

a fundamental source of happiness. It has brought us the financial mess we are in. We are hurt. The poor are hurt. The Third World is hurt. The Chicago School of Economics is wrong. To dig ourselves out of the Great Recession, we have to move beyond selfishness.

We have to resist the temptation to follow the crowd. If everybody else is cheating, we will be tempted very much to cheat. If everybody else is trying to live an ethical life, we will be tempted to live an ethical life. We were done a great disservice in the last thirty years by the School of Economics of the University of Chicago. Self-interest clearly played a major role in the economic crash. One good outcome is the discrediting of the idea that selfishness and greed are virtues. Let us move on with all the true grit and true gusto we can bring to the enterprise. Will secular or religious prophetic voices be raised in this cause?

CHAPTER EIGHT

Where Do We Go From Here?

It should be clear from everything said in the prior seven chapters that we Americans have overspent, have become too dependent on that spending for our sense of success and have embraced consumerism and affluence. The current economic downturn is not just a mere minor bump in the road. It is the major milestone. America has lost its economic prominence and many, many Americans are hurting financially and emotionally. And the gap between the super-rich and the middle class is widening.

These tough economic times are a spiritual wake-up call from which we can profit greatly. We can seize the moment and turn it into a great opportunity for reorienting our lives as individuals, as families and as a nation.

The question is how? That question is the title of this book: *How Does a Christian Profit from Tough Economic Times?* It is my hope that you will choose one or all of the following.

Simplify life by living within your means

The obvious meaning of this is that we have to sit down and figure out what changes we need to make in our lives so we are no longer regularly filled with anxiety regarding our debts and our bills. These bills include not only tuition for our children. They include payments on our house, payments for our car, medical bills, and payments for so many other things in our busy lives. Even if we can pay our bills, *we need to embrace the evangelical spirit of poverty found in the gospels and in Jesus' teaching.* With prayer, this alone can fill the emptiness of material possessions.

We start with ourselves, but know this requires an agreement among all family members, a concrete agreement as to the things that need to change.

Robert N. Bellah, the well-known sociologist at University of California at Berkeley, says it this way: "If both parents are working, and perhaps working for excessive hours, not to meet the basic necessities of life but to pay for what they think is a preferred style of life, (because of the pressures of consumerism) family life can suffer as consequence."

This is a nice way of saying that the *job culture* in our lives may be crowding out the *family culture*. I know this is a very hard thing to read. It seems so unfair. Perhaps no one ever asked you to do this before. Why not bring this insight to prayer and reflection for some time? You have to see if you can stop this to some extent. Economic pressures sometimes leave us no choice. And other times, they are accommodations which we have made to the allure of consumer goods which very suddenly have become "needs." That takes a lot of reflection, a lot of grace.

If materialism has eroded our religious and spiritual life, then it also has eroded the call to the *evangelical spirit of poverty.* You and I are neglecting self-discipline. So let us pray more seriously than ever before for the grace and courage to do what needs to be done.

Perhaps we need to slow down our lives so that we are not always in a hurry, not always in a rat race, not always on the treadmill. Perhaps we have to take enough time to read. Take enough time to pray. Take enough time for wisdom, love and friendship.

Help our children do the same

Our prayer and meditation also may need to focus on the culture our children are being brought up in. Is it simply a *consumer culture* or is it a *family culture*? A consumer culture is very often profoundly destructive of family life. So we will have to figure out how to teach our children self discipline, charity, empathy and all the other values that will help them neutralize the messages of advertising and marketing. Of course we have to model these values in our own lives as well.

Very sadly, a consumer culture says to our children that their identity is determined by what they have and what they buy. Very happily, a family culture of faith tells our children that their identity and ours is determined by who we are as a family, how we help each other and how we are related to God, our brothers, our sisters, our mom, our dad and our neighbors.

A consumer culture tells our children that buying is good and will make us happy. Our family culture says that buying needs to be moderated and will not make us happy for very long. What will make us happy for a long time is caring for each other as family and loving God. It even includes prayer and the sacraments.

Save for rainy days

Discernment is also needed to commit ourselves to saving for rainy days. The job culture surrounding adults says that the solution to life's problems lies in spending and purchasing material things such as trips, vacations and a big house. Our family culture says the solution to life's problems is trusting in God, helping each other and embracing virtue. If we do not believe in hard work and education, we won't make it.

Our job culture will say that a good life is a materially successful life. Our Christian family culture says a good life is a good family life and a life of virtue, love and service.

That involves saving for rainy days. Rainy days include sickness, accidents, loss of work and other things that suddenly befall us.

Pay down credit cards and other debts

Prayer and meditation will also call us to pay down our credit cards. Our children need to see us as a family working to pay down our credit cards every month. We need to think about "making our homes commerce free zones." That phrase was coined by the Institute for American Values. That means making a decision as a family to limit our use of cell phones, texting, TV, Internet, video games, etc. That means actively resisting buying the latest items right away. It may mean we will stop allowing ourselves and our children to become walking billboards for advertisers. It may mean engaging in activities that are not media driven and instead include volunteering together, walking, hiking, engaging in sports activities, etc. Paying down our debts is not just a small item, it is a huge item.

Practice frugality and industry

To sum it all up, we need to practice frugality and industry. This idea goes all the way back to Ben Franklin. Thomas Jefferson and George Washington are called the founders of American political freedom. Ben Franklin is called the founder of our economic freedom. He envisioned America as a place far different from across the ocean in Europe. It was to be a New World as compared to the Old World of Europe. In the Old World you could work all day every day, but as a serf or a peasant you usually couldn't pull yourself up by your own hard work and diligence. You could, in America, with industry (hard work) and frugality (live within your means...help your children do the same...save for rainy days). Ben Franklin received much of his thought from Cotton Mather, the Puritan preacher of New England.

Here are but a few thoughts from Franklin's *Poor Richard's Almanac*:

- Industry, perseverance, and frugality make fortune yield.
- Content makes poor men rich. Discontent makes rich men poor.
- Pay what you owe and what you're worth you'll know.
- No gains without pains.

The idea was simple and straight forward: if you work hard, save up for rainy days and live within your means you could be, as a family, free from all the terrible anxieties and heavy burdens that were a common lot imposed on the poor. He was not Scrooge. He believed a good life should come after you have saved, after you have worked hard as a reward. Ben Franklin believed we should sacrifice now for a future that involves the freedom from worries about where our next meal is coming from. By contrast, a consumer society believes that we should enjoy now and worry later. Consumer thinking is something that has helped bring us to our current economic crisis.

Franklin also believed (we should think about this) that children should fulfill household roles with the expectation that they contribute to the family by what they do every day. Social scientists today warn that such simple things as thumb sucking, ADHD, and many other maladies were close to nonexistent in families in Ben Franklin's day when children had to contribute to the family well being with hard daily work in the home and on the farm. Are they on to something?

Contribute to the betterment of our country

The practice of frugality and industry also has a larger purpose than serving just the family. When citizens heed Ben Franklin's wisdom, they pay their just debts, honor their contracts, keep their word, help each other in need, do not cheat each other and serve their country. This is called public virtue. And public virtue is absolutely essential for a democratic republic to flourish. In the 1830s, Tocqueville pointed out that the American experiment was an affirmative answer to this question: Can a free people, self-governed, exist and prosper without a monarch?

The French commentator, Montesquieu, whose writings so influenced the founding fathers, was convinced that a democracy was *the most desirable* form of human association but also at the same time *the least stable.* As long as a democracy, he said, is animated by public virtue, it will flourish. But *as soon as prosperity comes*, he said, public virtue tends to diminish and selfishness and greed take over. People cheat each other, don't pay their bills, don't honor their contracts, don't keep their word, don't help each other in need, and this happens at the highest level of commerce and finance and politics. Politicians and even ordinary citizens no longer serve their country.

Does that sound like what we have been talking about through all these chapters regarding our economic collapse? Too much prosperity in Montesquieu's eyes prompts temptations too strong for many to resist. In Montesquieu's mind, free virtuous people prosper. But then prosperity produces selfishness, greed and a laziness that affects the public business. Big business and government abandon the Golden Rule. Then people are no longer virtuous enough to govern themselves. So they give away their freedom in exchange for prosperity. They give power to a monarch who says: This is the saddest day of your lives. You did not have enough virtue to govern yourselves wisely.

Nadia Urbinati of Columbia University reminds us: "Uniting the globe so as to make all peoples partake of the same interests – and involve themselves in the same affairs does not make the globe more democratic or closer to a globalized democracy."

The job culture and consumer culture say that the primary goal in life is to garner material possessions. *Our Christian family life says that the primary goal is to love God and each other and bring each other home.*

Our Christian way of life says material things are means to an end and not an end in themselves. *Material surroundings must do what we want them to do instead of us doing what our material surroundings want us to do.*

It should be very clear that just as we need to live more frugally, the poor need to be helped to live more humanly.

We (all of us including our politicians) must consistently reject the mantra: "I want it all. I want it now." We must work hard to reject the greed of a self-interested capitalistic society, "the unquenchable thirst for temporal possessions." In other words, more and more is not better and better. To say that another way, we Christians should not be inclined to look with great favor on the worship of Mammon.

We need to pursue the good life, even the prosperous life, but we put God first. This means not pursuing the good life at the expense of our neighbor in need. This means living by the Golden Rule. It's the most neglected rule in life today! We must refuse to abandon life at any stage of its development. We do not believe in socialism. We do not believe in unfettered capitalism.

Our hearts must be obedient to the Lord in terms of the use of money, material possessions, goals and dreams. The Lord intends to redeem the whole world, to redeem all of us as a people and even to redeem the economic realities of our lives.

In the past, the economics courses we took in universities were individualistic (how do I make a lot of money with little or no thought given to how my individualistic economic goals impact others, both near and far). Individualism was a characteristic of the Age of Enlightenment, but relationality in economics is what we need today. We need our economic and political leaders to think of the betterment of the worlds' poor just as much as our betterment.

The Lord is our goal. Our real wealth is our family and relationships! Faith, hope and charity are our priceless possessions. Praise of God is our wealth. The whole Christ, head and body. We live in an increasingly pagan culture which needs to be Christianized. We need to integrate our religious values with our financial values and our community values and the time to begin is now.

Rham Emanuel, at the start of the crisis, was White House Chief of Staff. He quipped: Never waste a good crisis. He meant it in a political sense. Let us mean it in a spiritual sense.

SELECT BIBLIOGRAPHY

Altman, Roger. "Globalization in Retreat" in *Foreign Affairs*. July/August 2009.

Altman, Roger. "The Great Crash, 2008" in *Foreign Affairs*, July/August 2009.

Berle, Adolph A. *Power*. New York: Harcourt, 1961.

Blue, Ron and White, Jeremy. *Surviving Financial Meltdown*. Carol Stream, IL: Tyndale, 2009.

Bonhoeffer, Dietrich. *The Cost of Discipleship*. New York: Macmillan, 1966.

Bremmer, Ian. "State Capitalism Comes of Age" in *Foreign Affairs*. July/August 2009.

Cartlidge, Edwin. "Of Money and Morality" in *The (London) Tablet*, May 15, 2010. A Report on the Pontifical Academy of Social Sciences meeting on April 30, 2010.

Crocker, David and Linden, Toby. *Ethics of Consumption*. New York: Rowman and Littlefield, 1998.

Danner, Peter L. *An Ethics for the Affluent*. Lanham, MD: University Press of America, 1980.

Day, Dorothy. *The Long Loneliness*. New York: Harper, 1952.

Dilulio Jr., John J., "Risky Business: Golden Rule" in *America*, May 31, 2010.

Easterbrook, Gregg. *The Progress Paradox: How Life Gets Better While People Feel Worse*. New York: Random House, 2003.

Ehrenreich, Barbara. *Bright-Sided: How the Relentless Promotion of Positive Thinking Has Undermined America*. New York: Henry Holt, 2009.

Elgin, Duane. *Voluntary Simplicity*. New York: William Morrow, 1993.

Ellul, Jacques. *The Technological Society*. New York: Random House, 1964.

Frank, Thomas. *One Market Under God*. New York: Random House, 2000.

Franklin, Benjamin. *Poor Richard's Almanac*. New York: Skyhorse Publishing, 2007.

Fishman, Steve "Burning Down His House" in *New York*, December 8, 2008.

Gelin, Albert. *Les Pauvres de Yahve*. Paris: Les Editions du Cerf, 1955.

Grelow, Pierre. "La Paurete Dans L'Ecriture Sante" in *Christus*, 8, 1961.

Hammerslough, Jane. *Dematerializing: Taming the Power of Possessions*. Cambridge, MA: Perseus Publishing, 2001.

Hardwired to Connect: The New Scientific Case for Authoritative Communities (A Report to the Nation from the Commission on Children At Risk sponsored by the YMCA of the USA, Dartmouth Medical School and the Institute for American Values), 2003.

Hughey, John. *The Holy Use of Money.* Garden City, NJ: Doubleday, 1986.

Hsu, Albert, *The Suburban Christian.* Downers Grove, IL: InterVarsity Press, 2006.

Jones, Arthur. "Morality and Meltdown: An Interview with Christopher Lowney" in *National Catholic Reporter,* 45, May 15, 2009.

Kavanaugh, John Francis. *Following Christ in a Consumer Society*: Maryknoll, NY: Orbis Books, 1981.

Kinneging, Andreas. T*he Geography of Good and Evil.* Wilmington, DE: 151 Crosscurrents, 2009.

Lasch, Christopher. *The Culture of Narcissism.* New York: Norton, 1978.

Lenahan, Phil. *Steps to Becoming Financially Free.* Huntington, IN: 2006.

Lewis, Michael. *The Big Short.* New York: W.W. Norton, 2010.

Lowenstein, Roger. *The End of Wall Street.* New York: The Penguin Press, 2010.

Maslow, Abraham. *Journals of Abraham Maslow.* Monterey, CA: Brooks/Cole, 1979.

McKenzie, John. *Dictionary of the Bible.* New York: Macmillan, 1965.

Miller, Vincent J., *Consuming Religion: Christian Faith and Practice in a Consumer Culture.* New York: Continuum, 2005.

Mulhern, Philip: *Dedicated Poverty.* New York: Alba House, 1970.

Rahe, Paul A. *Montesquieu and the Logic of Liberty.* New Haven: Yale University Press, 2009.

Rand, Ayn. *The Virtue of Selfishness.* New York: New American Library, 1961.

A Report to the Nation on Thrift (Institute for American Values), 2007.

Rivlin, Gard. *Broke USA.* New York: Harper Collins, 2010.

Rogers, Carl. *On Becoming a Person.* Boston: Houghton Mifflin, 1961.

Schweiker, Wm and Mathewes, Charles, eds., *Having Property and Possession in Religious and Social Life.* Grand Rapids, MI: Eerdmans, 2004.

Snyder Belousek, Darrin. "Greenspan's Folly. The Demise of the Cult of Self-Interest" in *America.* March 30, 2009.

Teresa of Avila, *The Interior Castle*. New York: Doubleday, 1972.

Tett, Gillian, *Fool's Gold*. New York: Free Press, 2009.

VandenBroeck, Goldian, Ednoir. *Less Is More*. Rochester, VT: Inner Traditions, 1996.